The Clout Smiths'

Social Media for Small Business Owners

Christopher Sanger

www.cloutsmiths.com

All trademarks, brand names and products are property of their respective companies. The Clout Smiths nor the author have any ownership or relationship to any of the brands mentioned in this book. Seriously, we have nothing to do with Southwest Airlines or Best Buy or any of the other companies mentioned here, so don't go getting any wild ideas. We don't represent them and everything in this book is a matter of opinion.

This book is not meant to be used, nor should it be used, to diagnose or treat any medical condition. For diagnosis or treatment of any medical problem, consult your own physician

This book is designed to provide education and entertainment on the subject matter covered. It is sold with the understanding that the author is not engaged in offering professional advice or service. If legal or professional assistance is required the services of a professional in the appropriate field should be sought. No warranties or guarantees are expressed or implied.

Don't sue us.

Copyright © 2011 Ranger Sanger LLC

All rights reserved.

ISBN-10 0615499090
ISBN-13 9780615499093

DEDICATION

To Julianna, without whom this book could not have happened.

CONTENTS

SECTION I WADING IN

Disruption? Smishruption. 3

Don't Knock the AARP 5

Using This Book 7

SECTION II MANDATORY READING

Rules 11

The Big Four 13

Behavior 15

    Talk to people, never at them 17

    Remember the power of apathy 17

    The web is democratic– autocracy will fail 18

    Your online presence is a store 20

    "United Breaks Guitars" 21

    The permanency effect 24

    Frauds will be exposed 24

    Chrysler has a potty mouth 26

    Kill the robots 27

Know thy medium 28

Don't be discouraged 28

Getting Prepared 30

Imitation is the highest form of flattery 30

Measure everything 31

Strategy vs. management 32

Picking a Great Password 38

Picking Your Medium 40

SECTION III FACEBOOK

Defining Facebook 44

Why Bother? 49

The Social Graph 52

Strategy Rehash 56

Getting Started 59

Content Creation 63

Building Your Graph 69

Back to the Like 74

Go! Go! Go! 78

SECTION IV TWITTER

Twitter Defined 81

Speaking in Twitter 83

But, Why? 84

 Vendor love 84

 Web traffic 85

 Your clients expect it 86

Getting Started 88

 Advanced account issues 92

How to Build a Following 93

 A note on personal Twitter accounts 94

 The first tweet 96

Best Practices 101

 Protected accounts 101

 O RLY? 101

 Broken attribution 102

 Protecting your tweets 102

  Address your addressee 102

  Overly promotional RTs 103

  Down with Foursquare! 104

  Shutup! Shutup! Shutup! 105

  Auto reply is the devil 105

A Case Study 106

The Tool Box 109

SECTION V MOBILE APPLICATIONS

Mobile Enabled Applications 115

Why Should I Start Using Yelp? 117

Lingo 119

Yelp in Person 120

Mobile Yelp 122

Bad Behavior 124

Dealing with Negative Reviews 126

Advertising on Yelp! 129

Hit It! 131

SECTION VI WRAPPING IT UP

Hit It! Dig In. Go Further. 133

ACKNOWLEDGMENTS

I'd like to thank Brett Stenson for his help with the cover art and Julianna for her edits and her patience. Thanks to my folks for resigning to the fact that I don't have a *real* job. I will always be grateful to Peace Coffee for having unlimited refills of their amazing coffee. And to the University of Minnesota, for making me unemployable.

www.brettstenson.com
www.peacecoffee.com

SECTION I

WADING IN

Disruption? Smishruption.

Media professionals have hashed over social media's impact. There is no doubt that social media is disruptive to mainstream organizations, media and power structures. We get it. We are reminded ad nauseam by eager news casters on CNN. They want Twitter to be the reason that Egypt's protesters have been effective, why the Iranian "green revolution" was (almost) successful, but when you look at the reports directly from the people, you see that more traditional organizing efforts are really at the heart of their successes. As Americans we want to help, but sans doing anything material, having contributed Twitter to the world is our nation's consolation prize.

The truth is, claiming that social media has been disruptive to the political processes of the world is dubious at best. The changes we witnessed in Iran and Egypt were driven by the young who *happen* to use Twitter. It's a classic case of correlation, not causation. The fact is, young people use Twitter, and young people also happen to start revolutions. Having a population bulge of young, educated men and women is disruptive, especially when you suppress them. Having a population who uses Twitter, on the other hand, is not disruptive.

What Twitter has been able to disrupt is traditional advertising. There is a number that proves it: 500,000,000,000 or 500 billion. That's the number of reviews consumers share with each other online, and most consumers trust other consumers first when it comes to purchasing recommendations. When making a decision, a consumer who has a recommendation from a friend is 90% more likely to buy according to that recommendation. Advertising in print, television and radio was effective simply because we did not have easy access to a reliable and open source of recommendations. You couldn't call up your neighbor every time you were making a buying decision, nor would you want to. That would be weird.

Because social media is, if nothing else, a transcript of social transactions between individuals, we now have records of product recommendations. A friend clicking the Like button of a brand is a tacit recommendation for that brand. So, social media is likely to have implications for the purchasing decisions of other people in that person's network. Similarly, as brands integrate social media's new technologies, these recommendations are transmitted all over the Internet while still being intensely personalized. Imagine shopping online for a pair of boots. At one site, there are traditional marketing techniques: editorial photos, compelling copy, sex. At another site, you see that your close friend, an early adopter with great taste, has liked two products. Which site would our consumer be more likely to buy at? Of course, they will purchase from the site that has the approval of their friend. This isn't unrealistic either. The technology exists today and is easy to implement.

The disruptive nature of social media to advertising comes from its ability to deliver reviews and recommendations at opportune moments. This becomes more powerful as our social media goes mobile and the point of sale influences can be delivered in real space, real time. This is how consumers are engaging companies now, and it will only grow in the future. New media tools are no longer just for the brands with money to experiment; they are for everyone.

The tools available have never been cheaper and easier to use. They have also never been so confusingly abundant. But as a small business owner, you are already operating at an advantage. The small business is nimble and has a closely knit staff. The small business is energetic and exciting. It's embedded into the community. The small business has what it takes to excel in social media marketing, just by virtue of being a small business.

Don't Knock the AARP

Recently, I was on a conference call with the director of an internationally celebrated emergency medical system nonprofit and its office staff. We were talking about the various methodologies of fundraising and their efficacies. I wanted to help them launch a new and exciting initiative in their New England office. What struck me, and what I wanted to help remedy, was the institution's complete absence on any social medium. My hardest sell to the group was that launching a Facebook page could not only increase awareness, but expose them to new groups of potential shareholders, donors and opportunities. The hang up came from the fact that most of their current donors were in their 50s and they felt this key demographic was the only group worth targeting. (My words, not theirs.) It was time for a SWOT[1] analysis.

The problem with such a mindset is twofold. First, just because your current stakeholders and benefactors fall into one demographic doesn't mean that others wouldn't contribute if they were given the tools to do so. Thirty-somethings also donate money and time, so do twenty-somethings, teenagers and forty-somethings. In fact, in its fund raising campaign for the Haiti earthquake, the American Red Cross received donations from 3 million unique donors via text message. The Red Cross considers its key demographic to be baby-boomers, but you can be sure that the money raised via SMS forced the Red Cross to take a second look at Gen X and Y.

---

[1] Strengths Weaknesses Opportunities and Threats, a classic business school planning tool.

The second problem is that the notion that 50-year-olds aren't on Facebook is dead wrong, and it's getting more wrong. Social network use doubled for people over age 50 in 2010, and now nearly half of that population is on some form of social media. The other hard to ignore fact: the people turning 50 next year. They were 49 last year. Same thing for the year after next. As time goes by, this demographic will continue to be more and more connected with Facebook and Twitter and whatever new technology comes out simply by the process of aging. These people don't see themselves as old, and they certainly don't see themselves as too old for Facebook.

I didn't mention the name of the organization I was talking to not because they asked me not to, but because I wish them the best. I don't want someone with an AARP card getting angry with them because they believe their "key demographic" is too old for social media.

Using This Book

As you can see, social media has tremendous potential for marketing and brand awareness. Best of all, it's free, can be accomplished in just a few hours a week and as a small business owner you already have what it takes:

    a. You've got personality.
    b. You're organized.
    c. You understand the importance of networking.
    d. You're tenacious.

From my experience in small businesses, these four points separate the professionals from those who aren't going to make it. They also describe everything you need to build, launch and maintain a killer social media advertising campaign. With personality and just three hours a week you can go from having a mediocre web presence (or none) with no traffic to a full-fledged social media campaign. You don't need to know HTML, SEO or FMBL. You don't even need to know what they mean. You don't need a computer savvy nephew. You don't need a programmer. You certainly don't need to pay someone $90 an hour to do this for you, but I'd be happy to help if that's what you really want. If you do know about HTML or SEO, great. We will build advanced skills throughout the book. If you've never tweeted or updated a status, no problem. This book will walk you through the very first steps.

Back to those bullet points and your personality. You know that as an entrepreneur most of your business comes from the fact that you can relate your brand to people. So the "social" in social media shouldn't be much of a hurdle for you. Throughout the book you'll see this referred to over and over again, the importance of personality. Even when a case study isn't explicitly about personality, it's implicit. The "media" in social media exists only to broadcast that personality, to allow people to connect. Both the "social" and the "media" will be talked about in this book equally. I know you have the "social" down, and so do many others. That's why you'll often see guides for small business owners that omit the "social". Not here. The social aspect is too important and too intricate to be taken for granted. It's being applied in an area that's new for all of us. The rules our parents taught us for behaving in public can often be temporarily misplaced when exploring these new realms.

This book is meant to be a guide book. Think of it not as a novel or a how to book, but rather as a travel guide to a collection of destinations. That's how you'll get the most from it. By looking at the section at hand, you'll only be burdened by what's the most useful to you at the moment. A guide to Europe will cover the views on time in Spain and Denmark. But if you're going to Spain and plan on taking it easy, why would you read about the Danes? You plan on showing up for dinner 45 minutes late. The Danes would rather eat road kill than be late, but who cares? You'll be in Spain. We will cover best practices for Facebook and Twitter, two totally different beasts. We will also cover Foursquare, Yelp, advertising and return on investment. We are going to cover huge amounts of information here, but don't worry. You've got a leg up, and when you hit the ground, you'll be running with good form.

Another thing you might notice if you've read any other books about social media, besides that they left you needing another book (thanks guys), books lump social media together and treat the various sources (Facebook, Twitter, YouTube) as generic. This book will separate them because they are inherently different tools. They are used differently, for different purposes and are consumed differently. I like to think of Facebook and Twitter as a hammer and a wrench: both tools, both useful in their own ways. You could even use both to pound down a nail, but it's going to be a lot harder to pound down a nail using a wrench and you're going to look funny doing it. We're going to make sure we're using the right tool for the job so you can be efficient and produce something of quality.

Christopher Sanger

SECTION II

MANDATORY READING

Rules

It's easy to get bogged down in details, especially when dealing with something as complex as social networking. We are, after all, covering the social mores, technologies and systems that govern social media. Just to be sure that everything goes smoothly, we need to lay down some ground rules for dealing with social media. The reasoning behind these rules will be explained in detail in later chapters. The purpose behind them is to ensure your success as well as your continued sanity.

1. No more than 3 hours a week total on social media.
2. Delete your personal Twitter, or stop using it.
3. You are your brand, in real life and online. No anger, hate or bigotry.
4. Seriously, no bigotry, it *will* ruin you.
5. Politics will also ruin you, so leave it out.
6. No more than two social media outlets to start.
7. Measure everything.
8. No "auto" anything.
9. Don't worry.

If you take a minute to look over those rules, you should notice that most of these are pretty much applicable to being a successful business person in real life (IRL for the hip kids). Would you spend more than three hours a week of work time chatting with friends? Not if you wanted to get anything done. Do you bring your personal life into the office? Into sales meetings? I hope not. Three, four, and five apply to business and the dinner table. This isn't just about making money; these are to be a successful, social human being. Six is all about not overwhelming yourself and not getting bogged down in the details while making sure that your Return on Investment (ROI) isn't diluted by spending too much time on your social media campaign. Seven is all about making sure you get the highest ROI. Eight is back to that personality stuff. Remember your leg up? The last thing you want to do is cut that leg off by sending out zero personality form letters to people trying to start a conversation. And, of course, nine: Don't worry. You really can do this, and you can do it well.

The Big Four

Okay, now that that's out of the way, we can get into the fun stuff, social media. First we need to look at the playing field and identify the key players. We will look at their strengths and weaknesses and build our starting lineup. And that's the last sports analogy you'll see in these pages.

I could spend the next hundred pages listing all the choices of social networks that exist out there, most of which didn't make it into this book. There's a handful of reasons they aren't here. For example, you aren't going to find Tuenti here. Tuenti is a popular social media site, but it is not included here because it won't do you any good unless you speak Castilian Spanish and you work in Spain. You see, Tuenti is huge in Spain and is completely unheard of in the US. There are similar sites with unmatched popularity in Japan, Brazil and countless other nations. This book isn't going to be translated, so I doubt discussing them will do you any good.

There are too many "owned" media channels out there to be able to concentrate on them all. It's inefficient and, really, impossible to reach out on them all. Instead, we need to be strategic about where we choose to advertise. Gays.com is also very popular, but I wouldn't suggest spending time on it unless you specialize in LGBT weddings or own an LGBT bar. Even then, I find spending time marketing on such niche sites dubious. This is primarily due to crossover. Gays.com users have a very high likelihood of also having a page at another, bigger, social networking site. Another reason such sites won't be listed here is there just isn't space in a book for that kind of hypersegmentation. Wikipedia (another form of social media) isn't included here because I don't think it's going to make you much money, though I did use it as a source. The list of formats for social media is endless, as are the players in the game. It goes on and on. And on. Instead, we are going to focus on the big four.

Facebook, Twitter, Yelp and Foursquare. We will also dedicate tons of website space to email marketing, your website and some great web 2.0 tools. These don't count as social media, so they all go on the blog at www.cloutsmiths.com. All the chapters will have the same basic outline of what, why and how. What is the service? Why should you use it? How should it be used? All of which will be followed with a nifty glossary.

The big four were chosen based on a few basic factors. First, usership. They are all either already huge or growing rapidly, and they are all heavily used in the USA. There's not much point in focusing on a service no one has used since 2006. Sorry, Friendster. Second, they all have back-ends built for businesses. The days of the social media manager prognosticating results by divining rod are over. All these services are building powerful applications for business users to track and measure *everything*. (Remember rule seven?) This is also going to be useful if you aren't the owner of a company but an employee. You'll be able to use these tools to show you're not just goofing off on Facebook, but making your boss valuable contacts and building exposure! Even though, if you follow rule one, you're probably still spending most of your time goofing off.

Behavior

Before we decide which outlet you will be using, we will get some basics out of the way. Just like in the real world where some things just aren't cool no matter where you go, there are global rules and social mores for social media.

If there is one unifying principal to success in social media marketing it is this: marketing has shifted from broadcasting to conversation. This is the basic foundation for all the networks we will be covering here, and it's also the foundation for their rules. The success of this medium rests on some very basic human needs and desires. People first started grouping at MySpace in August of 2003 for the same reasons that people started grouping around a grain mill in paleolithic Mesopotamia. As Lewis Mumford, a preeminent thinker on the nature of cities, puts it: the things that brought people to stay in one place for the first time in history "relate[s] to a more valuable and meaningful kind of life." This is precisely the function social media sites fulfill. They are the new infrastructure of interaction. They are adding a new layer of meaningful social interaction. Users are able to create digital communities, replacing goods and services traditionally consumed in the public realm in a setting and tempo that suits them. This becomes especially evident as users turn to Twitter to ask for technical support or Facebook to request price quotes.

Just as social media's foundation is created from basic human needs, its rules also rest on some very basic human traits. These will form our new set of online social mores. But, keep in mind, just as the Spaniards and the Danes view time differently, users of different online communities have different sets of conventions. These rules have evolved from the different organizations of the communities.

The following rules are ones I have found to be global. Here again, you should recognize these as a professional practices. These are basic human traits that have been translated into a new medium. Some of them may not be quite so obvious, but they too are rooted in the same sets of centuries old rules. They are just dictated by the differences in data transmission and the virtual architecture of our new social media venture.

If you don't already have a great product, this may be the time to put this book down. No amount of PR, marketing or hype can save a disappointing brand. Remember New Coke? New Coke had the advantage of millions of dollars and an unsinkable brand behind it. I'm just guessing here, but most of my readers won't have that kind of clout. However, New Coke was trashed in publishing outlets and in the board room with abysmal sales statistics, not by millions of annoyed customers. If the Internet as it exists today had been around (important caveat since the Internet has been around since circa 1970), New Coke would have fallen faster than The Gap's ridiculous attempt to ruin their logo.[2] Instead, New Coke lasted seven years. If you have a bad product, the more successful your social media campaign the faster your bad product will die. Fair warning.

Social media is going to allow you to consolidate your connections, not moderate them. Consumers will shout from the rooftops if your product is amazing. Similarly and more reliably, if it's awful they will burn down the rooftops, bomb the village and drag you out Mussolini style. The following rules will help you contextualize all this, but social media is only a tool and it can't fix

---

[2]Here the logo lasted exactly one week before it was killed. http://www.huffingtonpost.com/2010/10/12/gap-gets-rid-of-new-logo_n_759131.html

something that's broken. As my former design teacher was fond of saying: "You can't polish a turd." Smart man.

Talk to people, never at them

It is important to find ways to continuously engage the user with rich content so they are not only thinking of the brand, but evangelizing it. By giving users good, interesting content you empower them to share their feelings toward your brand. Talking at users instead of talking to users comes across as an annoyance, and users now have the power to silence such annoyances and ignore them. People came to cities to enrich their lives, and users grouped online to do the same. One of the great advantages to living in an early city was shared knowledge. One of the great advantages of the Internet is that we can ignore anyone with the click of the button. (note: I mean silence to you, yourself, as in ignore. We can literally silence *nothing* once it's on the Internet.) Unfortunately for you, that means if you are perceived as being annoying for just one second, you're toast. Your message is spam and that user never has to hear from you again. You're broadcast message has been fed to the garbage. This is a conversation, never a lecture.

Remember the power of apathy

Barriers to entry in the digital world are magnified. I was once lucky enough to take a class in New York City with two well known interaction design professionals, one of whom designed Monster.com. They showed the class two designs for a website, one of which had one additional mouse click to complete a form. There was a difference between five and six mouse clicks between them to make a purchase, everything else was exactly the same. The design with five mouse clicks had an 85% completion rate; the site with six had 50%. In the industry, this is known as cart abandonment. Adding one more mouse click, a time difference of possibly one second, resulted in a 35% loss in sales. Amazing, right?

While we aren't necessarily building a site to sell things here (a web marketplace) you are selling something. You are selling your brand. You need to make it as easy as possible for users to engage with your product or company. By doing so, you enable users to share with others what they know about you and your brand. This requires thoughtfully placed entry points for all your media. Your website should connect to Twitter, your Facebook page should connect with your website. Don't expect users to go out of their way to do anything for you. Something about a person's attention span changes in front of a computer screen. I know I start to freak out when my music player takes more than 2 seconds to load. I froth at the mouth and curse at a website when it loads slowly. I've been known to throw my phone when an application takes too long to load. I don't know what happens to me, but it's not pretty. I know I'm not alone, either. You need to know about this ahead of time for creating content so you don't set your expectations too high.

Too many people enter social media thinking it will be a panacea for content creation. Users will flock to your site to create your new advertising campaign and provide you with copy and photos. Your marketing problems have been solved! It's not gonna happen without some serious shepherding. Even with serious shepherding, it's not likely. Bearing in mind the barriers to entry and the apathy you have to cut through, you can leverage your user base to create great content for you, but the perceived reward will have to match the perceived effort.

The web is democratic – autocracy will fail.

Free speech! If there ever was a rally cry for the Internet, that's it. It's an open dialogue, and just like people lost all patience in front of a screen, they lose all ability to moderate. Just hop on any news website that allows comments (most do, it keeps users coming back) and look at the comments on a political story. Go ahead, do it now... See what I mean? You can bet 99.95% of those people don't talk like that in real life. I've been involved in email threads about political issues, where *I knew* the authors of the posts, and they would never ever say the things they wrote in that thread.

If you choose your forum right, and avoid those non-dinner conversation pitfalls, the above shouldn't worry you too much. But you do need to be aware that people will post both positive and negative reviews of you. Some of the negative reviews might be absolutely bat-shit crazy. But your users are smart. They'll see something written by some crazy person and recognize, "Hey, that's a crazy person." Thusly, they will not take the advice of the crazy person. Interestingly, bad reviews can even be good for the perception of your brand, but only if the spelling is good. Studies have found that products with some negative reviews often out sell products will all good reviews as long as they are grammatically correct. Zappos recognizes this and has hired copy editors to clean up spelling and hanging participles in the site's reviews.

There will also be some legitimate criticisms. Just like in the real world, if someone criticizes your business and has even a sliver of truth or sense behind the criticism, genuinely thank them for their input, compensate them and fix whatever caused the problem. In doing so, you can improve your company's operations and turn a negative experience into a positive one. When such a criticism is posted in social media, don't delete that comment. I know you want to. It stings, and you're worried people will see it and write you off because you screwed up once. Don't do it. First, you can respond to that commenter like you would in real life (hopefully, as described above) and that will be visible to other consumers online. It will show that you care about your company and you take criticism seriously. Remember that part about your users being smart? It still holds. Your users will see a legitimate negative review and realize the other reviews are also legitimate. All viewpoints are then represented, and that shows authenticity being built.

Deleting a negative review will have some other negative consequences. Hell hath no fury like a reviewer spurned. It takes about 15 minutes to write a negative review on 15 different websites that link to you. You don't have control over all of them. In fact, you have control over very few of them. Be thankful your negative reviewer engaged you somewhere where you can make your response public. And remember, once something is out there on the Internet, even if it's deleted it's still out there and will be forever.

If you're not the owner of your company and you're still interested in joining Facebook and getting paid to promote your company, this is another great reason to do so. While you won't be able to control conversations, if you manage to build a positive environment for people to praise you *and* to haul you over the coals, you will be able to respond publicly and practice some damage control.

Your online presence is a store

If you build it, they *won't* come. If you spend all your time and money on fixtures and making your storefront attractive without offering anything for sale, they won't come. If you set up under a tarp and try to sell crappy products above MSRP, they won't come. It's about finding balance. Luckily, you're a small business, and I doubt you're going to drop 5k on an online marketing firm to offer your products for sale on Facebook (social commerce). Just like opening a new physical store, social media management takes work (albeit much less), It takes time for word to spread and it takes marketing. It's also a reflection upon your brand, so don't setup under a tarp. Expect things not to go perfectly for a month, expect hiccups and expect customers to take time to find you. Do not expect miracles and *be wary of anyone who promises them to you.*

"United Breaks Guitars"

Channeling conversation, listening and having a good product. These are the factors that will ensure you have a positive environment for discussion. People are more likely to post bad reviews than good reviews, a simple fact of human behavior. The goal is for the one good review you get from 100 satisfied customers will outweigh and *outnumber* the one bad review from 10 dissatisfied customers. If you can't pull that ratio off, you might want to reevaluate your product.

People are also more likely to syndicate bad reviews because people are more likely to put more time and effort into them than good reviews. They also tend to be funnier and more entertaining. How do you make a good review funny? Would Gordan Ramsay's show be a hit if he was talking about great restaurants instead of hell holes? I kind of doubt it. People also tend to get pretty creative. Creativity can reach the point where one small-fry guy can bring an entire multinational company to its knees. Case in point: the song "United Breaks Guitars."[3] If you haven't already seen this, I highly recommend it. I worked for one of United's competitor airlines at the time this video came out. It actually became company policy to take special care in handling guitars. They were to be placed into the cargo bin last and hand carried if possible instead of going onto the conveyor belt. That's not the kind of reactionary policy I'm advocating here – clearly if you have to react like that to a song something else is wrong in your operation – but it's worth noting that a YouTube review of United resulted in industry wide changes in what is surely one of the hardest industries to change anything.

On an unrelated note: did you know that if the spring loaded door that covers the trash on an airplane is broken, that plane can't

---

[3] http://www.youtube.com/watch?v=5YGc4zOqozo

leave the ground until it's fixed? It's considered a fire hazard. Since the spring loaded door, in theory, would cut off oxygen to trash fire and thus smother it, that bathroom is then missing an important piece of safety equipment. Next time your flight is delayed, consider that and just how many stupid things might be causing your misery and be nice to your gate agent.

Social media exists to amplify the consumer voice, positive and negative. You will have to take the good with the bad. It's this transparency and democratic narrative that has made the medium so appealing to customers, encouraging them to consume and produce content. A product that doesn't suck, or in economic terms is not an "inferior good", should have no problem with this. Just like a hilarious video from X Company can go viral, so can a video by a disgruntled airline passenger.

"United Breaks Guitars" is an example of a high impact, high circulation video, and there are others that run the gamut on impact and circulation. Another example from the airline industry: Kevin Smith. You may know of him for dark comedies like *Mall Rats* and *Clerks*. Smith was kicked off an airliner because they said he was too large to fit into a seat. He tweeted about South West Airlines's decision to deny him boarding and his fans went rabid. South West is an airline known for customer service, has an NYSE ticker symbol of LUV and once had a flight attendant go back through security for me because I left my hat at the ticketing desk – even though they knew I was flying a different airline. Smith's story made it to TV but didn't make the same waves as "United Breaks Guitars." The reasons for this vary, but I think it's because Smith's story wasn't what Chip and Dan Heath would call a "sticky idea." They wrote the book on that concept, so I'll refer you to *Made to Stick: Why Some Ideas Survive and Others Die* to learn more on sticky ideas. I recommend it, and I would consider making it the next step in your advanced marketing education. Smith, by the way, has since lost 65 pounds, so he shouldn't run into the issue again.

If you live in Minnesota or are a serious foodie, you might have heard of Isaac Becker. He's a world class chef and a James Beard Award nominee. He also happens to be the chef behind two of my favorite restaurants. If you like to turn your brain off after work, and I don't blame you, you might have heard of Bob Harper. Harper is the trainer on *The Biggest Loser*. Harper was in town, and Bar La Grassa, as usual for a Saturday night, was booked solid. Harper had the American Express Concierge service call and try and get him a reservation (a great service by the way), and AMEX was denied. The Bar La Grassa host respected that other people had reservations and was not going to "lose a reservation" because a demi-celebrity wanted some of the best pasta in the Midwest. I applaud him. Harper did not applaud him. Instead, he committed Twitter assassination (Twittercide?). Here's the tweet, right from Harper's feed. Keep in mind that Harper never actually spoke to the manager at Bar La Grasssa, only AMEX did:

OMG!! The manager at Bar Lagrasa in Minneapolis was SO RUDE to me. I wanted to have dinner there. Why are people so mean sometimes? ⌧fb7:41 PM Jan 22nd via TweetDeck

The floodgates were opened, and Harper's 130,000 followers showed how unhappy they were. Becker had to spend his Saturday night in the back room talking on the phone to angry Harper fans. Mind boggling.

Fortunately for Bar La Grassa, Harper is small potatoes and this quickly blew over, but not before making the papers and being syndicated across the Internet (more on that next). On the upside (for me), I went to the restaurant two weeks later and could tell the staff was on their toes. It was one of the best meals of my life. Clearly, the impact was pretty small overall. Becker won't be shuttering his windows – but it was a major annoyance and it ruffled the restaurant's feathers. This story is probably a realistic worst case scenario for most readers and doesn't sound like fun. But because Bar La Grassa was on Twitter they were able to respond. Because Harper gets filed under the Bat-Shit Crazy category, I'd venture to classify this one as "all publicity is good publicity."

The permanency effect

Web syndication ensures that just about everything posted on the web never dies. Once, I posted a link to my employer on a popular design website. The next day, I looked up all the sites that linked to us. That link, on that site, was syndicated to *tens of thousands* of sites. Part of the definition of going viral includes the virus's permanent introduction into the system. Even if it's a weak virus, it's still out there somewhere. Once someone publishes something, anything, relevant to anyone – even if it's just one person – chances are it's going to spread. Once it does spread, it ain't going anywhere. This works for things you want to go viral, as well as things that you don't want to go viral.

Frauds will be exposed

There are all kinds of schemes out there for business users to rack up huge amounts of followers, friends and likes. In a typical example, marketing company X guarantees to bring you 1,000 "targeted" followers on Twitter in three weeks. They then setup a Twitter account under a name of someone other than you and request 30,000 people to follow them. Once they get their 1,000 followers, they change the name and the keys are handed over to you. Do you really think those 1,000 people who chose to follow someone they don't know and don't care about will be high quality leads? Uh, no. They aren't going to follow you long, and you just wasted $200.

If you're tweeting for your brand and it's just you, don't say you're a team. If you're a team tweeting for a brand, don't pretend to be just one person. The users you want are high quality. That means they are paying at least a very small amount of attention and are somewhat intelligent. It doesn't take much to spot a fraud on Facebook. It doesn't take much to spot a business owner writing good reviews for themselves on Yelp. It's just downright unethical to give false bad reviews about a competitor. When you're found out, you're going to look like a fool (and a jerk). Don't forget, this is a small world. Despite all this Internet stuff, people still talk in person.

Chrysler has a potty mouth

Now it's time for an example that breaks all of the above rules with disastrous results. Chrysler has a boring Twitter stream. Go ahead and look at it if you want. The best tweet I've seen from them was, "We're having a good day, how about you?" Um, great? But it is a good place for fans of the company to group and share their enthusiasm. In what could have been marketing gold, the company fired off this tweet: "I find it ironic that Detroit is known as the ⌧motorcity and yet no one here knows how to fucking drive." Wow. Just, wow. This tweet nicely coincided with the company's retention of one Eminem as a spokesperson. While I wouldn't advocate swearing on Twitter, this was sure to get a lot of attention. And it did. Within seconds the tweet was made permanent and was retweeted and shared all over the Internet, there to stay – forever. Next, Chrysler revealed itself as a fraud. In the typical hyper-daft corporate management style, Chrysler revealed that all the tweets it had published, all the conversations it had had with loyal fans, were in fact written by an outside marketing firm. The firm was located in Arlington, Virginia, not Auburn Hills, Michigan, and the tweets were written by a team of social media professionals, not someone from the assembly line. Adios connection with consumers, hello feelings of betrayal. Could they have handled it better? Absolutely.

Not long ago, The American Red Cross (which I volunteer for) made a tamer but similar faux pas with its Twitter account. The organization's social media expert (Can I have your job?) tweeted about her desire for a dog-fish head ale, something I can relate to at this moment. Not a big deal, but the Red Cross has a congressional charter and is pretty touchy about being politically correct. What pushed the social media expert's tweet over the edge was the word she finished it with: "⬛gettingslizzerd." Not your typical slang from your typical Red Crosser. Slizzard, in case you didn't know, refers to getting drunk and is commonly used by southern rappers. Oops. While the Red Cross also immediately deleted the post, it managed to save face by using some humor. Shortly after the post was deleted, this was released via Twitter by the Red Cross: "We've deleted the rogue tweet, but rest assured the Red Cross is sober and we've confiscated the keys." No, it's not a knee slapper, but it accepts blame and makes light of the slip up. A perfect response if you ask me.

Because the American Red Cross handled the incident with humor and grace, all parties involved were able to benefit. Dogfish Head was so thankful for the free publicity they launched a campaign on Twitter to "donate a pint to the red cross," pint smartly referring to blood. Even better, it launched the campaign with the hashtag "⬛gettngslizzerd." Had the Red Cross decided to publicly announce that the original tweeter had been fired and issued a formal (read boring) apology, nothing good would have come of the misguided tweet. Instead, both organizations benefited.

Kill the robots

Just because you have a tool doesn't mean you should use it. There are a handful of automators out there and you should not use any of them.

Twitter offers the ability to take all your Facebook content and automatically syndicate it to your Twitter feed, there is also the ability to go the other way. There are two major problems with this technology. First, it comes off as spammy. Facebook and Twitter have different limits on how many characters can be used for a post. This is especially important when syndicating from Facebook to Twitter. Any Facebook update that is more than 140 characters will be truncated and your message will come out looking like this:

A great tip for brides to be: if before the wedding you're just not sure and are experiencing some seriously cold feet, run...fb.me/2489hs
12:45 PM Mar 12th via Facebook

If your message doesn't make sense (not the case here) your message is only going to be ignored because of our lowered barrier to entry. If it does make sense, it might not say what you meant and you run the chance of looking pretty silly. Okay this one certainly won't be ignored, but it's structured like that to prove a point. People aren't going to click on that link to find out what the rest of your message is. In this case you look like a crazy person offering horrible advice instead of getting your complete message of "...run to your fiancé and remind yourself why you're there," across. I apologize for how saccharine that was.

There are also ways to automate responses to messages and follows. Typically people populate those with "Hi! Thanks for the follow. Watch for special deals here!" I really can't imagine a better way to let someone know you are ignoring them and couldn't care less that they made the effort to follow or friend you. Could you imagine a scenario where a potential client walked into your office and they were greeted with a price sheet and told to wait around until you had something interesting to say? In my ideal world, maybe, but that's just not going to be successful online.

Know thy medium

It's important to remember that these media are not independent of one another. While you shouldn't be cross syndicating your messages, you should be making it as easy as possible for users to find you from one medium to another. This also includes your website, which you should think of as a launch pad to all your other media. Facebook is leading the charge on bringing websites of their business users into their system. It also makes it extraordinarily easy to bring its system into your site. Take advantage of it. The goal isn't to drive users directly from your website to your Facebook page, but it is to get the user to interact with you on Facebook so they are then linked to you in a tangible and long term way. As you'll see as we discuss these networks in depth, they are all useful for different audiences, but also different messages and attention spans. A message can be shared across the media, but for each medium the message will take a different form. From short sound bite style, to long form articles, a message needs to be communicated to different users with different needs while reinforcing other touch points.

Don't be discouraged

Starting to use social media is like starting a business. It takes time, patience and stamina. Unfortunately for you, the risk and initial investment is small, so it's easier to say, "Screw it," and walk away. Don't do it. Stick with the program. Follow these rules, be yourself and know your medium. If you do those three simple things, you'll build a whole ancillary network to help you sell your product.

I know it's hard, building the web presence and communities and keeping up with them to promote this book has been daunting. I've spoken with other full time content creators, and they all say the same thing. Stick with it, no one may be listening at first, but if you make enough noise for long enough someone is bound to start paying attention. Just remember to keep your time relationship with social media to a manageable level and keep plugging away.

Here's a neat statistic to motivate you: users who use social media have a network 20% larger than those who don't. And that's a real *old-school* "We talk to each other," network. That means that your network can grow by 20% and that the users you engage will have a 20% larger network. That's a pretty valuable group of people to have "like you."

Getting Prepared

It's time again for a reminder not to worry. Those were quite a few rules and some harsh examples. But I'm guessing you realized at some point that those are all things you do (or rather don't do) in the real world. The basis for all those rules comes from old-fashioned sales sense, your social skills and a very basic understanding of the Internet. We just extrapolated them out a little. If you just keep your head about you, you shouldn't ever come up against one of those.

Imitation is the highest form of flattery

It's also the best way to learn. Get online and find a few businesses you admire. They can be anywhere in the nation, but I'd recommend finding a few in your city. Bookmark their pages on any of the big four outlets we discussed before, Facebook, Twitter, Yelp and Foursquare. Read the archives. Read the comments. Notice posts that get lots of conversation going and notice posts that no one takes the time to talk about. Write those posts down or copy and paste them into a document. You want to make a document where you can look at successful posts in one place. There is a pattern in there, and as a people person you should be able to tease it out. Make sure if one vendor doesn't have all four media you find a source for each one. This introductory step is key to you deciding where to focus your efforts. Notice on each medium who the audience is and how the audience interacts with the media. Pay special attention to the differences between the media. If you already know which outlet of the four you are going to concentrate on, just follow that plus one more. Give yourself something to work up to. If you're going to work on Facebook, get on Twitter as well.

Measure everything

Peter Drucker, the famous and brilliant management consultant, said, "What gets measured gets managed." The important part of that statement, I think, is its converse. That is, what does not get measured does not get managed. And you're a lucky duck when it comes to this rule. You stayed out of social media before following this maxim was even a possibility. The big four networks we chose to look at all allow you to gather in depth data about individual impressions, users, posts, interactions, just about anything. This will let you find what exactly is working and what's not so you can tweak your interaction accordingly. It's also these back ends that will allow you to measure return on investments. Social media have different inherent value in the actions taken by their individual users. It's this value that makes reading this book worthwhile in the first place. You need to capture the value of these media and turn it into revenue!

Everyone has heard of Groupon by now. There are a hundred similar sites: LivingSocial, DealStork, etc. For our purposes, these all constitute what's called a flash sale: highly discounted items available for a limited time. Another interesting example of a flash sale platform is ChompOn. ChompOn allows the prospective sale owner to set up a flash sale, only instead of relying on driving traffic to a website through email (Groupon) or word of mouth and membership (Gilt Group), ChompOn integrates with social media. Flash sales are then made available through Facebook and Twitter. It too has a strong backend that allows for some interesting metrics to develop.

Using its platform, ChompOn has determined the gross revenue generated by each action implemented by a user of a social media site. Such research is especially important as we try and nail down what you should be focusing your efforts on in the social media realm. Its methodology limited the value of each action to only the immediate next sale, so it's possible that the following table underestimates the value of each action. This is because it doesn't take into account their long term value. These values are also representative of a particular sale at a particular price, however, that I'm inclined to say the ratio will hold true for any price and over time.

Facebook Share $14
Facebook Like $8
Twitter Tweet $5
Twitter Follow $2[4]

There is a clear price disparity between media and within each medium different actions have different worth. So why bother with Twitter when Facebook clearly delivers a higher ROI? And why bother with likes when shares have so much more potential earning power? Well, like we talked about in the preface, each medium serves a different purpose, which should explain the disparities above.

Strategy vs. management

What is strategy and what is management? These are both words we all use often, but they are so nebulous that they are hard to define. Strategy is your goals and how you're going to get there. It's not the tools you'll use or the actual nuts and bolts of the operation. That's management. It's important to separate the two so you can adjust them appropriately. Is your management toolkit missing

---

[4] http://socialcommercetoday.com/facebook-share-worth-14-rpa-revenue-per-action-a-tweet-5/ The source of the pdf published by ChompOn along with a more detailed explanation of their methodology and pricing.

something, or is your strategy unrealistic? I've seen drastic changes in strategy to correct for poor management to detrimental effects. I've seen wild shifts in management because the company's strategy isn't clear. That didn't end well either. Knowing that your goals are not the same as how you'll get to them will help keep you from throwing the baby out with the bath water.

The definition of strategy I find most useful is an o... from 9 BF (Before Facebook, aka 1996)[5]. It works for the s... reasons that the other global rules work: social media is an ... of our existing social structure onto the Internet. Remembe... new way of interacting, but we can learn some things from ... we have been doing things here in the real world. The num... most popular article from the Harvard Business Review is b... E. Porter, and it is called "What is Strategy?" It's the most p... because strategy is so important and so easy to pass over. Ac... Porter, there are three key principals that you need to keep ... when defining strategy:

1. "Strategy is the creation of a unique and valuable position, involving a different set of activities." Or said in a different way, it's a definition of what customers a company will serve and what need of those customers the company will serve. An 'aspirational brand' like Louis Vuitton will not serve the needs of all the people all the time for carrying things. Instead it serves a small market segment and a specific need of that market. This is part of its strategy. The company is hard to imitate because it has a well defined strategy, which makes it a luxury brand.

2."Strategy requires you to make trade-offs in competing – to choose what *not* to do." Since Luis Vuitton sells luxury items, it only captures a portion of the market. If it were to sell a discounted

---

[5] Bad joke, I know.

line of purses it would probably manage to sell many more purses in the short term. However, in the long term Luis Vuitton might hurt the part of its brand that is aspirational, which will certainly hurt sales in the long term since its original market segment will abandon the company.

3."Strategy involves creating 'fit' among a company's activities." This just means that all activities should be mutually reinforcing. Luis Vuitton, along with hand bags, sells a series of books on travel. They are a very handsome set of books and come in a leather case and include listings for ultra exclusive hotels, fancy restaurants and fine art galleries. This reinforces the idea that you should take your handbag with you to these exclusive destinations. A bad fit would be the inclusion of a budget travel guide.

Perhaps most important in the article, we are reminded that employees need to know how to "deepen a strategic position rather than broaden or compromise it." Just like employees need help in this arena, often so do social media users. It's important to remember that social media is just another tool in your organization to further your strategy, and thus it must *fit* with your strategy. If you are able to make social media, and your voice within it, fit your strategy, it will reinforce your other operations, strengthening them rather than weakening them.

It's important that if you don't already have a formal strategy for your company that you sit down and devise one using the tools available to define your position within the market. Doing so will help strengthen your social media presence (and likely your day to day operations as well). Having a clear strategy will also allow you to pause before making any decision and ask yourself, "How does this help achieve my strategy?" This isn't to say that everything needs to be a single minded beeline to some abstract mission statement. That's no-fun corporate think. You can make posts online that might be completely irreverent, that have nothing to do with the strategy, but you cannot make statements that weaken your strategy.

The well thought out strategy is one that takes into account three points: uniqueness, trade-offs and how well it fits. These three points build a strategy that will define a company with a sustainable competitive advantage. Having a strategy will help you decide which customers to target on your social media. It will also help you avoid the confusion that many people find their media streams in when they try and target all people all the time. Such attempts lead to a bland or schizophrenic online brand presence. It also helps you avoid competition from other brands. If your brand has a strategy and operates according to it, your competitors would have to copy more than just an advertisement to tap into your market. In fact, they would have to copy nearly your entire business operation. This is because well thought out trade-offs and fit mean you are providing the best service to your market segment possible, since all of your business practices align to offer that segment the best service. In essence, a great strategy ensures a definitive audience while building a barrier to entry for competition.

It's easy to fall into the trap of primarily concerning yourself with management instead of strategy. Why? Because operational efficiency is more easily measured with minutes and dollars. Small changes are testable. It's the perfect way to occupy yourself with being busy for busy's sake instead of making your company awesome. Which brings me to the next point.

Be awesome! If strategy sounds like a bunch of management speak, and your eyes have completely glossed over, don't worry. Just be awesome. Pick the customer you want and do everything you can to be awesome for them. In his Awesomness Manifesto, also for the Harvard Business Review, Umair Haque proposes that we ditch the idea of innovation and instead focus on being awesome. I couldn't agree more.

Harque has three main points that parallel the points needed to create a strategy. First, create insanely great stuff. Build things that people will need and want and do it well. Love your job and make sure your employees do too. If your employees love your company, they will be empowered to represent it well and authentically. If you love your work, your personality will show in your work and your work will reflect your personality. If someone loves your company they can be the perfect spokesperson.

It's also easier to build further greatness into a company you love since you know its strengths and how to play into them. A final part of awesomeness is *Thick Value*, or making value that "is real, meaningful, and sustainable. It happens by making people authentically better off – not merely by adding more bells and whistles that your boss might like, but that cause customers to roll their eyes." Tom's Shoes is a company that lives and breathes *Thick Value*. Its strategy and mission is reflected in nearly everything it does. Tom's gives away one pair of shoes to a needy child for every pair that is purchased. It doesn't give away shoes to make money; it makes money to give away shoes. The company is structured so that its values run throughout the operation. The value is not a veneer. It is very clearly the company's purpose. This is Thick Value.

You can't make an awesome product without trade-offs since an awesome product can't be all things to all people. A product that tries and fails to fit all people, inevitably, is the opposite of awesome. All things to all people means a product won't work great for anyone. Instead, if you're lucky it will be acceptable to most. Awesome products will also fit your brand since an awesome brand and the people who work for it will do everything possible to expand that awesome. Finally, an awesome product speaks for itself and is hard to duplicate. Anything later will be an impostor, not a more affordable version or an alternative. [6]

Develop the big picture and focus on it. Make sure your employees know it. Make doubly sure you know it. Social media will allow you to present your strategy to your customers in a very real way and will help them understand why your company is the best company on earth. Knowing your strategy will result in a consistent voice throughout your social media and will allow you to easily engage your users. It will prevent you from posting boring things. Write down your strategy and keep it handy. Reference it whenever you are going to post something on a social medium. Take a Post-it and put it on your computer screen to reference whenever you are interacting with social media. It should ask "Is this awesome?" If you ever answer anything but "yes," try again.

---

[6] I've always wanted to write a paragraph that included the word "awesome" seven times.

Picking a Great Password

Before you even start on a network we need to talk about passwords. Selecting a password is one of the most important and under-considered things you will do throughout this process. Most people use easy to remember people, pets, dates, objects, etc. Pet names are particularly popular and also happen to be one of the easiest passwords to crack. Anyone who knows you, anyone who can see your Facebook profile, anyone you meet can very easily find your password when you use such information. It can happen to anyone. It happened to Brian Dunn, the CEO of Best Buy. Dunn's 5,000 followers, employees and customers all saw him tweet, "I'VE BEEN HAVING A LOT OF GREAT SEX LATELY AND HERE'S WHY..." followed by a link to what he assumes was a site selling performance enhancing drugs of a specific type. His password was stolen. Don't let this happen to you.

There are a number of steps you can take to prevent someone from finding your password. The first is avoiding what the Department of Defense calls a "single guess" password. Any word that could be guessed by the hacker on the first guess should be avoided. Thus, anniversaries (can be found via public records), pet names (you'll offer it) and family names (How often do you talk about your kids by name?) must all be avoided. Basically, the rule of thumb is to avoid any whole word that can be found in a dictionary along with names and dates. However, combining things from this list can yield an effective password. Combining a daughter's name with her birth year, "Sasha1997," is far and away a better password than either alone. It's still not a great password, though, and can easily be compromised by a site that offers password reminders.

Adding length, symbols and numbers are the most effective ways to build a strong password. Microsoft recommends starting and ending a password with a symbol. I sometimes find it useful to convert numbers to their corresponding symbols on the keyboard. So, let's add Sasha's birth month and day onto this password, using the symbols associated with the numbers and see what happens. The 26th of May could be added at the beginning to make @⊠%Sasha1997 (265 for May 26 = Shift+265 = @⊠%).

Another favorite technique is to take a phrase and convert it to TXT speak. Not only is most of it completely incomprehensible to most adults, but when strung together it's likely to lose all meaning. The website lingo2word.com offers a text to speech converter that can do most of the work for you. If your existing passwords don't fit the bill, change them now. Even if you have an awesome password for your Facebook page, your account is still at risk if your email password is the street you live on. Why? Hackers can easily find your email password and not use it to send out email of their own. Instead, they sit on it, silently. They can read your email and find out all about you while requesting password reminders from all the other sites you interact with: bank account logins, social media, frequent flyer numbers, your gym schedule. The list is endless. Change your password.

Picking Your Medium

From here you'll pick your medium, and then it's choose your own adventure time. Your first time through, I recommend starting with one medium. Concentrate on it for a few weeks. Once things start to go smoothly and you've found your groove, feel free to add another. You should begin to pick up momentum as you move through these sections. Learning about social media is like learning a language. Once you learn one, the second, third and fourth are progressively much easier. Until you reach a point where you're able to manage both systems in just two hours a week, don't move on. This is supposed to be a small part of your business that's earning a large return. If you're spending all your time on social media, you might as well be going out and meeting prospective clients the old fashioned way.

This list is ordered to my preference, I've taken into account both the amount of time you'll need to invest, potential ROI and ease of entry or learning curve.

1. Facebook – It has the most users, it is the easiest to use, has the most robust back end and chances are you're already using it. It also offers the cheapest, most effective advertising on the Internet.

2. Twitter – It is great for B2B relationships, not so great for getting new clients. It has a smaller user base and not as many ways to interact with content. It offers a great stage two program, though it will take a decent time commitment. This is my number one choice if

you sell directly to other vendors and they make up more than 50% of your bottom line (or you want that to be the case).

3. Yelp – As a business owner, you get some pretty great tools to measure returns, announce specials and respond to praise and criticism, but not much else with this medium. It's worth keeping on top of, but that shouldn't take much time. If you're in stage two and are looking for another medium but don't want to spend much more time managing it, this might be a good choice.

4. Foursquare – Yelp incorporates some of Foursquare's features, but theirs is a worthwhile application. It seems every time you turn around Foursquare has added new features for the business owner.

There's one more group of social networking applications I want to mention before going on: the business application. LinkedIn is the gold standard at the moment of apps for the professional. I have a profile; you probably should too. It's just a nice way to keep in touch with professional contacts and be found by headhunters. It's very low maintenance. I visit mine maybe once a month to update publications and current project status. There is very little that can be customized and you have to follow its format. The low maintenance and the minimal thought required to make a page is probably why it is such a successful medium for professionals. It's basically set up like an online resume and should really follow the same rules as a real paper resume. That's why I have no desire to go into LinkedIn in this book. Writing a good resume is an art form, and opinion varies on how to do it best widely. That's a different book. LinkedIn can also be used for headhunting, and for that purpose I recommend it highly. Job seekers can send you their LinkedIn profiles instead of their resumes, the hiring manager gets a great look into their lives. The users profile isn't as filtered as a real world resume and people tend to be more candid.

Look over this list, take a look at what friends and competitors are doing and make your selection. It is an ordered list, and I'd recommend starting with number one. If you already have a Facebook page, still read the Facebook chapter and decide if you are doing everything you should be. If you are, move on. Don't worry if most of the rules in this section went in one ear and out the other, the rules will be referenced where appropriate but in less depth later in the book. If you ever need clarification just flip back here.

SECTION III

FACEBOOK

Defining Facebook

Facebook is big. It has massive amounts of data on each of its many users, and hordes of new users sign up every day. Yet, it escapes being unwieldy. It wouldn't if the people behind it didn't spend so much time making sure it seems so simple. The amazing thing about Facebook is despite the sheer size of the network and the amount of information it contains, how intuitively it functions. It all seems organic. But when you sit down to define all the moving parts that make it tick, it can get tricky. There are so many pieces put together that don't exist anywhere else.

This is an *attempt* to define all those moving parts. At least, the important ones. There is no doubt this won't include everything, especially since this is a book and things change but these pages do not. Read over these, preferably with Facebook open so you can read the description and identify its counterpart. If you don't already have an account, now is the time to sign-up. This part might get tricky, even if you do have an account. It's going to be even trickier to keep your concentration in this chapter. Trust me, I know. Every time I go onto Facebook to fact check something I end up spending 20 minutes there. This took forever to write. If you don't have one, start a personal account. You'll need it to get a page for your business anyway. It's simple, just head to www.facebook.com and dive in. But come right back, okay?

Profile: If you're an average American Internet user you probably already have one of these. (If, despite the last sentience in the last paragraph, you still don't, please sign-up for one now.) This is an individual's digital stand-in on Facebook. It is what they will use to interact with the network. It allows for privacy, requires a users permission before another user can interact with it and is how users see other users. It condenses and displays information about the actions, interests and connections of the person on Facebook.

Page: This is what a business should use to interact with Facebook. Very much like a profile, it functions as the digital stand-in for the business on Facebook. It condenses and displays information about a business. It is specifically designed for businesses, so it works differently than a profile. There are different privacy settings on a page, and the owner of the page doesn't have to approve the interactions of others with it. It also comes with powerful analytics and some fancy features we will cover later – like interfacing with FBML and the Open Graph Protocol. The page's main function is to facilitate open communication and to allow users to interact with it. If there's nothing else you take away from this chapter, remember that point. Defining the purpose of a page to facilitate open communication is why we design and interact with the page the way we do. Remember the concept of free and open communication and ask yourself when you're on your own, "Does this encourage free and open communication?" Those questions will never steer you wrong.

The News Feed: If the Facebook profile is a user's home, this is where he hangs out. After logging into the system, this is the landing page. It is designed to display content generated by the interactions of others within the system that the user will be interested in.

There are two main parts. The first is top news, which is the landing page for every Facebook user when they visit the site. It's ruled by a complex algorithm called EdgeRank that is based on how often a user interacts with someone or something, how recently they did so and how valuable that content is ranked to be. For example, if you have 200 friends and "like" 30 pages (a pretty average user) and you interact with 15 of them on a regular basis (average) it shows that those people are probably most interesting to you. This is what Facebook calls affinity. These 15 people you interact with often then have a high affinity ranking and will compose, say, 80%[7] of the content displayed in your feed. The other 20% will be composed of the other 215 contacts you have.

The News Feed is Facebook's most powerful distribution channel, and it's your goal to be in as many news feeds as possible. This is a very basic attempt to explain EdgeRank since it doesn't take into account objects or the multitude of other ways an object can be valued to a user. An example: if User 1 likes a movie and someone they never talk to on Facebook also interacts with the same movie, there is a very real possibility that the interaction will show up in User 1's feed. This is another example of affinity.

Another portion of the algorithm is weight. Facebook basically ranks content as follows: 1. Photos 2. Videos 3. Links 4. Status 5. Applications. Within those categories, posts where a user takes the time to write something is given higher rank than posts generated by applications or a third party. The final element is time, a post's value decays as it ages. This will be important to remember as you decide when to post your content.

This will be covered more later where the specific parts are important, but for now it's important to understand that the more a user interacts with something, the more it will be shown to them and that different types of content (movies, text, photos) have different weights within the EdgeRank algorithm. The News Feed isn't random, and since we know that and basically how it works we can use it to our advantage.

We aren't going to try and game the system, that almost always ends badly. Technology companies spend ample amounts of time and money making sure that those who are gaming their systems are quickly stymied. For an example just look at Google's responses to

---

[7] Based on personal observation.

"black hat" SEO, or marketers who try to game their search algorithms. Try as they may, they are quickly found out and Google adapts to punish their efforts. Instead of gaming the system, we are going to try to understand it and create content that will follow the rules EdgeRank imposes on us.

The second view of the news feed is called "all news." Roughly 50% of users click over to the all news tab, and here, all content generated by all connections to the user is displayed. EdgeRank does not apply here. This is like a news ticker or Twitter, with data arranged chronologically and without discrimination. Something worth noting: if a user has very few friends or connections they will therefore have very little data to filter. This means their top news and all news feeds will be very similar, and your post is less likely to be filtered from within top news.

Facebook has a complicated relationship with privacy settings. The company is constantly berated for having too much information on its users and for its data policies that sometimes appear sneaky. Facebook has, in the past, implemented new features that resulted in huge amounts of new data becoming public. But on the large, it recognizes the need to respect privacy and has come up with a set of privacy settings that allow the user to make very detailed decisions about what will be shared and what won't. This fine grained approach to privacy is part of the reason Facebook is such a hospitable environment for the personal user. They have also learned from their past product roll outs and now seem to strive to make new roll outs less disruptive to users information sharing preferences.

The news feed freaked people out at first. It was, after all, aggregating data about all of a user's connections and displaying them. It was called a virtual stalker. Now it's why people use Facebook. It redefined the way people interacted with the network. It made data more permeable and more relevant, both traits that made Facebook seem less private while making it more interesting to users.

Part of the reason it was able to make this transition was the implementation of those in depth privacy controls.

The Wall: Instead of a news feed that aggregates content about a user's friends, the wall collects data about a user. It lists everything a specific user has said or has had said to him (within the bounds of their specific privacy settings). It is located on the user's profile and it's the most viewed page of anyone's profile. It is where the action happens. For example, if someone interacts with your brand's page, it will show up here as an object. Objects from users' walls are then selected based on Edge Rank to be placed in their friends' news feeds. The original Facebook was just a collection of walls, and all users did was browse through them, interacting on individual walls. The news feed has changed this, and now users interact with individual walls less frequently, but they are still a very important part of the experience.

Why Bother?

Five hundred million users is why, and that number is growing every day. Pretty much everyone and their mother is on Facebook. My mother's mother is on Facebook. I was having a conversation with friends, and every single one of us had a grandparent on Facebook. It's impressive just how deep and wide our online networks have grown. Facebook is clearly fulfilling a human need in a way that is impossible in physical space. But just as it's creating new possibilities in a new space, it's also creating new rules and new means of interaction that we are just starting to tease out. I'm sure a decade from now this paragraph will seem quaint, and I'll be glad this book was published for a small enough market that few will have read it.

Five hundred million users also means that 1 in 13 people on earth are using Facebook, and 72% of Internet users in the US are on Facebook. We crossed a point sometime in the early 2000s where your business had to have a website. An Internet presence was no longer an ancillary marketing activity. It became a mandatory part of doing business. In fact, sometime in 2010 users became more likely to turn to their computers to find phone numbers or hours than our bulky yellow friends. I personally haven't had a phone book for at least five years. Customers are now accustomed to looking online for directions, hours and news instead of looking in the Yellow Pages and making a phone call. If you didn't have a website, customers were going online, trying to find your hours and navigating to your competition. It became a sign of a lack of professionalism not to have a website, and it cost you money. We are crossing that same line with Facebook. People are now spending more time using Facebook than they are checking their email. People request price quotes on businesses' pages. A Facebook page is no longer something that shows your company is innovative and young, it has become expected. But that's not to say your page itself can't be innovative and interesting. It has to be. It's another form of advertising, and you wouldn't approve an ad you thought was stale or uninteresting.

Facebook pages also allow the customer to become acquainted with your brand in a way they would not otherwise be able to. They allow you to accentuate the uniqueness of your business, letting the customer form an emotional connection to your company. This is possible with traditional advertising, but not easily achieved. Once a customer forms such an attachment they are no longer just a shopper or consumer. They are part of your company's team. A surprising number of people who like a brand on Facebook (around 40% surveyed) do so just to show brand affiliation. It's much cheaper to like Puma on Facebook than it is to buy a pair, and customers know it. In an age when individuals define themselves so heavily by what they consume, it's absolutely essential to provide the ability to your customers to link themselves to you on the world's largest network.

Remember how Facebook has huge amounts of data on its users? You have access to a whole lot of it. Since Facebook now claims such high membership and branding interaction has become so pervasive, Facebook's analytics application, Insights, has become a powerful indicator of both online and real world trends. For example, Insights will allow you to find out the ages, sex and locations of your users. Basically, a panacea of demographics research for your company. This information can be wildly helpful for you to identify trends, customer needs and desires to more narrowly define your company's positioning strategy.

A final reason that will pop up throughout these pages is search engine optimization. Google uses Facebook when computing where in its ranks your brand will show up. You want to be at number one. Using Facebook is a good free way to boost your search results ranking. Google Analytics now includes social actions and social engagement data for administrators to track how social their content is.

Even if Google and Bing and all the other search engines don't use social actions for ratings, which is totally possible, they do use link frequency. The more pages that link to your site, the better the site does in search engine results, it's the most basic part of the algorithms they use.. So, the more your page is shared, the more links are generated, the more traffic you get.

The Social Graph

    The following five unique actions are part of what Facebook calls the social graph, or the network of connections with which people communicate and share information. When thinking of the graph, try not to think of a pie chart or bar graph. Instead, think of a complex network of links like a spider web. Individuals more familiar with computers and networking know that those links are called nodes. These individual nodes spur off connections to other nodes, and this linkage between nodes creates the core of the social graph. Those linkages look very much like edges and that's where the name for EdgeRank comes from. By ordering the values of the edges created by users, Facebook can decide which links are most valuable and display them to users, who are then also more likely to value them. It's also very similar to the way the Internet is structured, one link spreading to 5 more and onward exponentially. Another way to think of the social graph is as an ecosystem, with many complex moving parts all connected to one another to create one large, functioning system.

    Another part of the Facebook ecosystem is the object. Objects can also make connections with nodes and each node. An object is any discrete piece of data published in Facebook's ecosystem. It could be a user's interaction with information about a movie that creates an object, or it could be a user sharing a news story about Egypt. Either way, it means that user, or node, is attached to an object, which is also attached to the original creator of the object, as well as anyone else who is interested in the object. Simply put, an object is a thing and a node is a person, place or business.

The idea of a graph is an allusion to the way Facebook sees its users interacting with the medium and an indicator of their long term goals. Facebook is a graph at its core. It's a way to show and explore how people and interests are connected. The graph does not move from Point A to Point B to C. Instead, it's connecting Point A to all other points that point A might share something in common with. In the long term, we see Facebook trying to make data easier to interact with, easier to integrate into their system from disparate sources and easier to connect between nodes.

The following is a list of the terms that define how users interact with the social graph and how it is displayed. These are important because each action has different weights associated with it, a different level of effort required of the user and a different payoff. Knowing what it means to tag, share, like, post and comment and how to leverage them will allow you to move your brand onto Facebook in a useful and meaningful way. It will also help you make money.

The Like: This is the most common action of Facebook and also the lowest barrier to entry for the user and the lowest level of engagement. This is like giving someone a digital thumbs up (hence the icon). Much of the effort spent by social media managers is trying to coax users into liking content. What does a Like mean for you? It means your brand will show up on the liker's profile and that your content will also show up on their wall. Hopefully it will also show up in the top news feed of their friends, but this is determined by EdgeRank.

There are new and exciting developments that have taken the "like" and elevated it to a new level. It's now able to accomplish so much more by interfacing between your website and Facebook, you and your user. It's important to know that the Like is easy to implement and is the most basic way Facebook users interact with the graph, but it has advanced functionality that can boost your interactions to the next level.

The Share and Send: The Share is essentially a long form Like, and with the advanced functionality of the Like that's available, I think the Share's shelf life is limited. However, for the basic user it is still a very high value action, and even if the Share disappears, the function of the Share will be rolled into the Like or the Send. Similar to a Like, its content is generated from a Share button implemented by the original content owner. The Share takes an object the user decides to share, allows the user to comment on it and publishes it on their wall as a full story. The send does the same, but acts more like an email sharing the object as a private message. This compares to the basic functionality of a Like, where the object is published as a one line blurb with very little information. The user is also prompted by the Share button to add their input to the story, thus building its affinity ranking.

The Tag: This is really the highest value, the highest barrier, to entry action a user can take. A Tag means your user was thinking of you independently and took the time to tag you in a post they wrote from a Facebook page that was not yours. There is no button they clicked on your site to tag you, there was likely no prompting by you to get them to tag you and in all likelihood their tag is going to show up in their friends' news feeds.

The Comment: Commenting is also beginning to change forms. Like the Share, the advanced functionality now available means there are new and exciting ways to implement comments across the Internet.

The Comment can mean comments directly on your website that interface with Facebook. It has become exceedingly easy to place such comment forms directly on your website and, this marks a powerful thrust toward Facebook's move toward interfacing with the rest of the Internet and bringing that data into its network.

The old and still very relevant forms of comments are those found directly on your page. These come in the form of a user commenting directly on a piece of content you publish. If you update your status, post an image or share a link and a user shares his or her thoughts on it, it will show up on both of your profiles. Also, because of EdgeRank, if a user comments on your status and another user they are friends with also Likes your business, the story generated by that object will also show up on their friends' news feed.

That's a whole lot of jargon real fast, isnt it? Put another way, if Tom Likes you, and Sue Likes you, and Tom writes on your wall, a story about Tom writing on your wall will likely show up in Sue's top news feed.

Understanding the different objects in the Facebook ecosystem will allow you to use them to put your brand in front of your consumers' faces. Best of all, you can do it for free.

Strategy Rehash

Facebook provides new ways to reach your customers in intimate and personalized ways. Fifty percent of 18 to 30-year-olds check their Facebook first thing when they wake up.[8] It doesn't get more intimate than a customer browsing your offerings in their underwear. That also means 50% of your target market, if you play your cards right, can be looking at your brand first thing when they wake up. This is where Facebook's strongest marketing possibilities lie. Facebook brings you into the customer's comfort zone and the user tends to interact with the brand more like a friend than a sales person. Because of this, it's important to keep in mind that Facebook is rotten for advertising in the traditional sense. Facebook isn't the place for the hard sell, and if you try, users are going to get annoyed. They are expecting you to behave like a friend and not a salesman. However, if you give your users the tools to sell for you, they will be the cheapest and most effective sales people you've ever had. We will develop these ideas and how to tap into the *brand evangelist*.

The reason we aren't able to advertise in a normal 1830s-2005 sense on Facebook is because Facebook operates in a plane between the public and private. The conversations that take place can be intensely personal, but they are taking place in the most public realm possible. This is part of the reason social networking sites can be so dangerous for young people. It's hard to differentiate what is acceptable use of a system where boundaries are so ambiguous. Most *adults* have a hard time with such obtuse concepts. This is probably

---
[8] Internet Statistics Compendium EcoConsultancy

why 20% of divorces are now citing Facebook as the precipitating cause. If it's that challenging for an adult with 30 years of social experience, how can we expect someone trying to navigate middle school cliques for the first time to grapple with it? That ambiguity of privacy is also why people get so annoyed when you advertise to them here. It's seen as invasive.

You don't get mad when a telemarketer calls you at your business. It's expected and it's within the realm of where business gets done. Okay, I get mad, but not nearly as mad as when they call at other times. Compare this to the dinner time telemarketing call. The call that breaks into your family time at home. A personal time. This is why it's so frustrating. And now with cell phones, telemarketers can find you *anywhere*. This is the most frustrating of all telemarketing calls, because now they can break into an intimate conversation you're having on a first date. So, when your hard sell shows up in between two close friends on their news feed, one sharing vacation photos and one their recently ended relationship, it's going to come off as an intrusion.

If the hard sell is not going to work on Facebook, is brand awareness all that can be achieved on Facebook? Is there more? Absolutely. Besides awareness, we can foster brand loyalty on Facebook in new and exciting ways. Facebook can help us find, cultivate and nurture people who love our brand and turn them into brand evangelists. This way, we can leverage the social graphs of our customers through simple, low barrier to entry tasks that will connect our brand to their network in a meaningful way.

The first step to any successful social media strategy will be a close examination of the normal operating procedures and existing advertisements of your brand. Remember, this is an extension of the existing advertising, not an alter ego. The voice of the company should be consistent with your brand in the real world. If your image is classy, stay classy. If you're a rag-tag team of goofballs, don't use Facebook to highlight your serious side.

Make a commitment to engage your users. If they came to your page just to get your hours, they are long gone. If they took them time to comment on your wall, they are on your page to get to know you and expect you to return the gesture. Because we know that we are on Facebook to foster conversations, build brand awareness and enable users to share your brand you can structure your strategy around these goals. Ultimately, your strategy will come down to how you use the voice of your company to achieve these goals while using what you know about EdgeRank to increase visibility.

The goal is to share useful, interesting, funny or generally engaging content with your users so they can interact with it as they choose. The content can take all shapes and forms, but the goal is to create one consistent voice that can act as your brand. Constancy is key, Facebook anthropomorphizes your company, and we don't want your brand to come off as boring or a schizophrenic. The easiest way to ensure a constant voice is to assign one person to be in charge of social media, across all platforms. Something harder to accomplish that requires some practice is avoiding the boring, but by following established rules for content creation, your engaging content ideas should come in time.

Getting Started

If you still do not have a personal Facebook account, it's time now to get one. You need to have one to move on. You have no choice. Dive in. (Make sure you have a good password!) Once you're logged into Facebook you can create a page for your business. Navigate to www.facebook.com/pages/create.php and choose Local Business. Follow the onscreen instructions and you're off. It's important to use a Facebook local business page instead of the other options available, like groups, a profile page, or a brand page. The reasons to avoid each of those other options vary, but they include limited features, lack of accessibility, friend caps, the need to manually approve friends and the fact that users can't like a profile. Another reason is that Facebook has created the pages function specifically for local businesses and have already introduced great features specifically for the business audience. It seems likely it will continue to introduce great features for businesses there, so it's all the more reason to start in the right place.

Facebook will walk you through most of the steps to create a basic profile, so those steps aren't outlined here. They do a good job, and attempting to explain the process will just date this book faster. However, there are things to keep in mind when setting up your page for the first time that will affect the basic way people interact with your profile. These are listed under Manage Permissions. Earlier, the importance of the wall was discussed, since this is where users interact with you and how they share with you and create objects relating to your brand. Many companies, unfortunately, choose to cut off the wall by removing it entirely or not allowing users to post on it. The fact is, this ensures that some of your highest value content will never be shared and customers will have no way to interact with your brand. If there is true concern about offensive comments, turn on the profanity filter and let your users do what they want. If something truly offensive pops up, just get rid of it and add the user to the block list. Note, however, that this is not a license to delete legitimate comments that may take issue with your brand, respond to them and turn the bad experience into a positive one for the customer. Rule one of customer service applies just as much online as it does in the real world.

Since the release of Pages, many things have changed, and the use of Facebook for businesses has evolved at a breakneck speed. Some very cool things have been happening that you should be aware of. One consideration is the ability to use Facebook for commerce. This is a huge development, and it means businesses can now sell products directly from Facebook. The idea here is based – at least partly – on knowing about user apathy. If someone is shopping for face wash and they are already on Facebook, Dove hopes that by keeping the user on Facebook it will be able to capture a sale.

There are two major problems with this development that I can see. First it reminds the customer that the only reason the company is on the network is to capture sales. Second, it pulls traffic away from the wall. Because companies are so eager to convert their fans to sales, they often change the landing page on their profile from their wall to their commerce page. This stifles conversation and again, alters the initial impression the user has of the Facebook page from conversational to a one way sales pitch.

Another consideration when it comes to setting up your profile is your picture. I'm never a fan of logos for profile pictures online. It's almost always best to go for a photo with people in it or at the very least a photo of your product, preferably an action shot. Logos are just cold, and they immediately tip off others on Facebook that you are a company trying to sell something instead of a person using Facebook that happens to work for a brand. There's a more in depth discussion on why it's better to be a person than a logo in the Twitter section because on Twitter you can only have one picture represent you. On Facebook you can post many pictures, and if you do choose to use a logo for your profile picture you should be sure to include other pictures with yourself and your employees elsewhere on Facebook. The best practice for this is to just throw them up on your wall, much like a status update. This way they will be cataloged, but will also be immediately visible to your guests. This is in contrast to loading them as albums using the image uploader, which will hide them in the photos section of your page. This is a difference between 3 clicks and 1, and we can never forget how much extra work one more click is for a user.

You should also be sure to change your profile picture regularly. Photos are great content, and the profile picture is the best place to highlight important content since it is the most frequently viewed image on your page. If you get new merchandise, highlight it here. People are more likely to look into a profile picture change story than a story about adding an image to an album. The profile picture also has the benefit of being nearly full size right on the profile page. Again, this creates one less click for the user, and you can be sure everyone who lands on your page will be looking at your profile picture.

Be sure to make that profile picture count! The ideal formula is a 200 pixel wide and 600 pixel tall image with an area of the image (200x200 pixels) that can be used as a thumbnail. That is the largest image that can be displayed full size as a profile picture on your page. This means more real estate on your page for more information and bigger impact. Take advantage by including compelling content for greater impact.

You are going to see FBML come up at some point while doing your own research on Facebook. FBML stands for Facebook

Markup Language, and it's a programming language that allows Facebook users to expand the functionality of their pages. If this is something you're interested in, check out Facebook's developer page. If it's not, and I doubt it is for the readers here, don't sweat it. Just know it's there. It's the fancy side of Facebook and it lets programmers sell their time to people like you at exorbitant prices, even though you don't really need it to have a good social media marketing campaign. Besides, most of the advanced functionality FBML offers can be had via free apps offered by kind developers. If there is something you want your Facebook page to do, just search for it. Chances are someone else made an app so you can do it for free. But don't get carried away! Too many apps make a page unnavigable and confusing.

Content Creation

You don't need a consultant or programmer or fancy FBML to create a high quality, high impact social media marketing campaign. Doing so is all about creating great content, and that's something anyone can do with a little practice and understanding of what good and bad content is. You don't have to be a copywriter to generate great status updates and you don't need to be a photographer to post great photos. In fact, most of the photos I post come right from my cell phone's junky camera. They are good photos because they let the user into the day to day operations of the companies I have worked for. Something you do day in day out may seem boring to you, but to someone who has never done it, it might just be the most interesting thing they learn about the day you post it, especially if you use photos to say it.

I'm a negative person, there's no doubt about it. I love to bitch and moan. It's an essential part of my sense of humor. But on Facebook or Twitter, I never hate anything. Negativity is dangerous territory. Unlike in private conversation, when you offend someone online by denouncing their favorite band, there's no way to talk your way out of it. It's also permanently published, there for the world to see. You never know how many of your fans love Justin Bieber, so bite your tongue.

There are some other things to avoid when writing content. The obvious are politics, religion and other social taboos. Less obvious are clearly self-promotional, spammy or robotic updates. These qualities all signal that your brand isn't available for the kind of connection the user is looking for. They also signal that you aren't worth following.

Great content has four main qualities, it's engaging, short, immediate and logical. There are many ways to be engaging. You can be funny, you can ask a question, you can be informative, off beat, shocking or thought provoking. The key is to provide something the user will want to read. Whenever you write anything you should stop and ask yourself: first, who is my audience? And second, will they care? Being engaging could even be as simple as saying, "Yes, I hear you," to someone who took the time to write to you.

Content should be short. Facebook allows you to write fairly long posts, but just because you have the space doesn't mean you should use it. Be pithy. The English language is full of junk words. Chanel your inner Hemingway. Or Twain, who wrote, "Substitute 'damn' every time you're inclined to write 'very'; your editor will delete it and the writing will be just as it should be." The average magazine reader looks at an advertisement for 3 seconds before moving on. While we aren't writing advertising copy, it's still important that your message can be read quickly. No matter how much I bemoan the fact that we live in a sound bite culture, it's completely true, and if you can't get your point across in one sentence, it's going to be lost on the masses.

You also need to make sure your content is immediate. This really means two things. First, it's timely. If you can inform your readers of something before anyone else can, it is high quality content and will build your users' perception of you as an expert and influencer. You also need to ensure that your content is immediately understandable. I've read too many updates you would need a decoder ring or a deep understanding of Proust to understand. Complex thoughts can be difficult to get across and harder to understand. Subtlety and sarcasm don't do well in short updates. If you leave a customer confused they will feel annoyed or, worse, stupid. A dose of truth: being funny in writing is hard. Very hard.

Just look at how many jokes have been compete failures in these pages. It's harder when you have to be positive and have such limited space to work with. Don't despair.

Second, be logical, duh. Make sure your posts make sense for your brand and for the medium. This goes back to the brand's voice. Don't break character. If your voice on Facebook screams fun, it's going to be strange if you start posting business advice. It also means remembering the rules of social media. Don't expect your users to go out of their way for you, and don't expect magic. Asking users to brainstorm new products for you isn't going to work. Asking for music suggestions may. It's a question of how easy it is for the user to come up with the information they need to answer the question. They don't have to wrack their brains to think of their favorite dance song, but to post a picture of themselves with your product takes considerably more effort. There needs to be a payout for such a high time expenditure, otherwise they just won't respond. It's important to remember, though, that asking for creativity on the part of the user is not the same as asking for feedback. It's like writing papers in school: the more open ended the assignment the harder it was to write. Here too, the more constraints you put on an answer the easier it becomes to answer.

Easy Feedback
We need to know what kind of music to play at our party. What's your favorite song?

Hard Feedback
We need a costume for our Halloween party. Post a photo of yours!

That's not to say it's impossible to get feedback when requesting it in the form of content, but the payoff has to commensurate with the difficulty of input. Even if you can match the payoff with the effort, these kinds of posts can seem desperate and contrived, (especially if they go unanswered). It's better in the long run to just let the conversations start organically. Once people start liking your brand and begin interacting with your page, they will start posting on your page and interacting with your posts.

However, as your fan base increases this becomes less true. The more people you have to pull from, the more likely some of those fans will be rabid enough to respond to even the most audacious requests.

As a small business you have a huge advantage over some of the world's most beloved brands, like Coca-Cola, which at this moment has 23.5 million fans. Well, you have an advantage on Facebook, maybe not in the soft drink market, but because you are small and local. This should figure heavily into your Facebook strategy. Users are far more likely to interact repeatedly with a brand that engages them locally versus a large brand like Coke that simply cannot do so. More locality simply means more relevance. This is especially important when we consider the importance of EdgeRank on our posts. It means the information will more likely be found in the top news feeds of your users, and because it's relevant, they will be more likely to interact with it further, boosting its EdgeRank and spreading your information further.

Post images, tag them and describe them frequently. Images are weighted much heavier than any other post format and are more likely to be syndicated with EdgeRank. They also receive more interaction from users than other posts. Your cell phone is great for snapping pictures since you always have it on you. You can post directly from the Facebook application to your page's wall. It's fast and easy, and it's worth doing. Posting is an art. There's no way around it. But as a small business your brand should have some part of your personality in it. Reflecting that personality should make perfecting the art form much easier and enable your success.

How often should you post? Go ahead and do a Google search on this and you'll see why I won't answer that question with a number. There are "experts" everywhere who put bogus numbers out there on how often you should post and cite some research they did independently without going into detail. Yeesh. The real answer is totally dependent on you and the voice you've established for you company. You want to strike the balance between engaged and annoying. There are too many variables to give a good answer for everyone, so you will have to navigate it yourself.

If you're a DJ you will probably want to post more than a company that rents tents. Why? You're perceived to be in the technology business. You are also constantly generating content, like which songs you're buying, which songs are popular, etc. I could see a DJ posting as many as five times on a heavy day and creating good content. I hope the tent rental company owner finds their job interesting, but I doubt the opportunity to create content and share is quite as easily available. But, maybe not! It's all about creativity here and I've definitely met tent rental vendors that are far more interesting people than some of the DJ's I've met. As a small business you also have the benefit of being personal, sharing about your life can be great content as long as it's not alienating.

In order to find your own ideal number of posts, sit down and schedule updates and posts for one week, two a day. Do this every week for a month. At this point, you should have enough data to look into your analytics and decide for yourself if you need to be posting more or less. Or, just have an honest conversation with yourself. Can you keep up that kind of output? Are you enjoying it? If not, you might want to scale back. If you love it, go hog wild.

As you get into your analytics you will also be able to determine the best times to post. This is important as not all of your users or fans will have your content show up in their top news feed. But, if you post at the time when most users are on, you will have an advantage. The advantage comes from two points. First, your content is freshest so there is no depreciation for being old. Therefore, it will be more likely to show up in the top news section. Second, even if your content doesn't show up in top news, if your users are online when you post, the content will show up nearest the top of the all news feed, which more than half of users click over to, making it more likely to be read.

With all that said, the number one rule is this: Don't publish crappy content. Ask yourself if your reader will care. Ask yourself if you would care. Use the active voice. The passive voice is boring to people. Passive voice bores people. See?

Building Your Graph

The very first step is to Like your page personally. If you have been using a personal account and have a group of friends there, hit them up. Be shameless. Once you get to 25 Likes you will be able to assign your page a static URL (like: www.facebook.com/yourbrand instead of an indecipherable string of numbers). If you don't have friends to hit up, email past clients, peers in the industry, your parents, etc. Set up an account for your dog and make him Like you – technically against the terms of service, but if Mark Zukerburg's dog has a Facebook profile, yours can too.

Once you have the static URL you can begin to leverage existing touch points to build your fan base. You're already in contact with your clients via email, you hand out business cards and you have a website. Each of those touch points should enable the customer to find you on Facebook and Like you. The website is the easiest for the user to transition from what they are doing (being on your website) to Liking you on Facebook (just one click). This is especially true now with the new functionality being implemented by the Facebook Development Team. If you have a blog, Facebook can be used to enable comments on your posts. You can even pull your profile from Facebook right into your website so the transition becomes seamless. A tool I recommend for building awareness and leveraging your email as a gateway to Facebook is WiseStamp. It works with most browsers and most webmail clients. It enables you to put a "stamp" at the bottom of every email with an image or text that links to your social networking sites. I also include my Twitter feed and links to Yelp and recently won awards on my WiseStamp.

Facebook's integration into your existing touch points is a two way street. While it's important to drive traffic to your Facebook page or objects from those existing touch points, we have to remember why we are doing so. For an illustrative example, Talking Points Memo's story *Facebook & TPM (Social Media Geeks Only)*[9] shows how after setting up a Facebook page, their referral traffic (people who clicked a link to one of their stories on Facebook and came to TPM's webpage) went from almost zero to their single largest source of referral traffic. There are two actions happening on Facebook that can account for this. First, people are sharing stories directly from TPM's site onto Facebook and those stories, published into their friends' news feeds, are influencing new users to come to TPM's site. Second, after people like a story they are linked to TPM's page. TPM's stories then show up on the liking user's news feed, becoming even more likely to be shared again as they are now part of the Facebook ecosystem. Since the user is already interacting with Facebook the barrier to entry for a share or like is lowered. In this way the viral loop is initiated and sharing becomes exponentially more likely.

Another great way to entice customers to Like your page or look deeper is to offer them content they can't find elsewhere. You might post something like a photo captioned, "Check out our new line! We're excited to be carrying it!" This would be a great example because it includes a photo, which is high value content, and it's also news about your company. Privileged information is a great way to lure customers in. Things like Facebook-only deals can work wonders.

Nearly half of the people who Like a page do so because they want a discount. A large number also stop Liking a page because they do not receive discounts from the company. This means you should

---

[9]http://www.talkingpointsmemo.com/archives/2011/03/facebook_tpm_social_media_geeks_only_1.php March 2011

probably offer discounts on your page, and since we can make them privileged discounts that only people who visit get, it's a double whammy. However, don't offer anything on Facebook you wouldn't want to offer every one of your clients. Small discounts are useful just to show you are offering discounts on your page. There is no need to discount heavily since doing so gives the impression that you will do so repeatedly. Existing customers will want the same discount and large discounts often draw in low value customers.

Another solid approach is the contest format. Keep in mind that technically you must use a third party provider to host a contest on Facebook. Small companies doing it on their own are frequently seen, though. Facebook has this rule because the laws on sweepstakes vary from state to state. It's also why I'm going to include this disclaimer: The following contests are examples of things I have seen. I am not endorsing either, nor am I recommending you do either of them. If you choose to host a contest, be sure to check state and federal laws and comply with Facebook's Terms of Service. A surefire way to avoid any of these problems is to use a third party provider like wildfire.com. Anyways, there are two basic approaches to the Facebook contest, what I call "The Like Mill" and the "Build For Me."

In The Like Mill, the brand defines a set time period and encourages people to Like the page. A prize is defined and at the end of the time period one person who Liked the page during the contest wins a prize. If you have company T-shirts or swag, this is a decent strategy since it requires little effort and you can assign a prize with a fairly low dollar value. This strategy is based on knowing that Likes do have a monetary value (some say as high as $18 each). This is a way to build up a following fast. The higher the prize value and the longer the window to win, the more Likes one gets. On the other side of the coin, the higher the prize value, the more likely you are to attract people who are only interested in your prize, not your company. This is why using branded material or a high value prize linked to your brand is important to the success of the campaign. Giving away cash or a trip to the Bahamas is a surefire way to attract a huge number of low value followers. Unless you sell trips to the Bahamas.

Build For Me is all about content creation. Here, a prize is assigned along with a time window. But instead of just asking for a Like, the brand is asking for the user to upload photos, videos, comments, ideas or whatever is deemed to be of value. These contests usually seem to be shorter, and the prizes seem to be of medium value. I like these contests more because they actually build the value of the brand's page by adding content versus The Like Mill, which just adds followers.

All that being said, I'd avoid the contest trap entirely. The followers they attract tend to be of low value and the chance of the user unliking the brand after they don't win the contest is high. It's like signing up for a credit card to get the bonus only to cancel it, something that has gotten this writer many free flights. An occasional small discount and constant good content will do wonders to get users to like your brand, and they will be high value users too. It's not as fast, but the results are better and cheaper.

Social ads are another very cool feature of Facebook. Because Facebook knows so much about its users, the advertiser is able to leverage that information to direct ads to very specific subsets of users, which would have previously been impossible. In the late 90s early 2000s with the advent of digital cable, advertisers were excited that they could target ads to specific zip codes on specific stations. Now, we can target female users who have recently become engaged between the ages of 22-26, a very specific demographic! One wedding photographer did just that, spending just $600 on Facebook advertising. He was able to directly link $40,000 to that advertising campaign. Try that with radio! These ads are hyper segmented and can be effective. They are also dirt cheap. In fact, they are one of the cheapest ads on the web in terms of cost per impression. Once you have a decent profile built up, with a month or so of posts and plenty of images, you can dive into Facebook ads. When that time comes, visit the blog at www.cloutsmiths.com and read over the most recent articles. I didn't include advertising here because it's changing too rapidly and is too segmented to go into a book.

It's also a good idea to get your employees on board with Facebook. It's hard to show employees you are a person just like them without crossing over from being the boss to being the friend. It's something most managers struggle with, and most decisions we make when interacting with employees are influenced by this line a manager must walk. Facebook provides a great way to connect with employees without crossing over that line – provided that you are professional on your page. It allows the employee to reach out and interact with you on a social level without the kind of commitment needed to do so in real life. It also doesn't carry the implications of interacting socially with an employee in the real world. That isn't to say one shouldn't be as vigilant of the self when interacting with an employee on social media. We haven't seen a case of sexual harassment brought to an employer via Facebook yet, but it's just a matter of time.

Facebook is already being used as evidence in such cases, and there is no reason it couldn't be the medium for such harassment to take place. Two women bringing about a sexual harassment case against their employer have had their profiles entered as evidence because the defendant claims that their claims of depression and emotional damage should be reflected on their Facebook profiles.[10] People have been fired for Facebook posts, students dismissed from school and teachers disciplined.

---

[10] http://www.lexology.com/library/detail.aspx?g=3bf92ed9-ea8c-41d9-bee6-c744f2042a17

Back to the Like

As mentioned earlier, the Like has advanced by leaps and bounds since it was first introduced. This is primarily due to the efforts of Facebook developers and their creation of the Open Graph Protocol (OGP). This name should make some sense since we already know what the graph is, and we know that Facebook wants the information elsewhere on the Internet to be able to interact with its network. OGP is simply the tool set Facebook has implemented to allow developers to bring in all that other data. This is what allows users to use their Facebook profiles to leave comments on news sites, review products or recommend stories to friends. It's how your Facebook feed can now show up on CNN's website. Since the Like's functionality has increased, it needed a slight rebranding, or maybe co-branding. "Recommend" is part of an effort to make the Like button more universal. Both Like and Recommend can be employed, and are basically the same. You can generate the code for either from the same place within Facebook's controls. You simply choose the verb when creating your button. The name change is due to the fact that it just feels wrong to *like* a story from the New York Times about genocide, whereas *recommend* makes sense.

The Like button, or Recommend, is the primary plug-in to interact with the Open Graph Protocol. It's very easy to implement and very easy for the user to take advantage of. It allows Facebook to read and write the local part of the graph that lives on a particular site. In other words, a Like button can now communicate in both directions with Facebook. It can create the object and call for the user to interact with that object without ever leaving your content. Every time a user likes something on the Open Graph, that Like adds data to the users Facebook profile. It also can provide you with valuable data about your users.

A simple idea of how to take advantage of the advanced functionality might be on the checkout page of your website. Say you're a photographer and you've just accepted payment from a client. They have either landed on a website that is their receipt, or they are sent an HTML email using a service that allows you to gussy up your email with images and dynamic content, like MailChimp. Either way, the client's receipt contains a Facebook object that could say, "Share with everyone that you just booked your photographer!" If the user clicked on that link, Facebook would then create an object describing the story, it would also link that user to you in a permanent and interactive way. Since you can describe what your object is, it can be placed within the users info section, becoming an activity, interest or one of the things the user is a fan of.

Implementing the Like button on your website is fairly easy and can be done using code readily available from Facebook. It's a simple matter of copying and pasting. The code can be found under the marketing tab of the edit your page function. When implementing the Like button on your page, there are a few things to be aware of to maximize your click through rate, or the number of people who choose to Like your page or post. These tips, according to Facebook, increased the click-through rate of sites that used them by 300% to 500%. First is including the thumbnails option for the Like button. When the user is logged into the Open Graph, this option displays profile pictures for the friends of the user who also clicked the Like button on that page. This brings the user quickly into your community since they can see both their profile picture and the profile pictures of their friends who also like the story, increasing credibility.

Allowing the user to comment on the Like before posting is helpful to both you and the user. If a user comments on a story, the object will be published as a full story and will have higher edge rank because the story was user generated instead of coming from an application. This is because it is user generated, not created by an application. It also allows the user a certain amount of control over the content, increasing their sense of ownership, which will then make them more likely to post. The friends of the person that liked the link will be more likely to have the story show up in their feeds and will therefore be more likely to share it themselves. Letting users share their two cents is clearly in your best interest.

A second tip is to include the Like button at both the top and bottom of the story. This is due to the lowered barrier to entry. If someone is at the top of your page and wants to Like your story, they are not very likely to scroll to the bottom to see if there is a like button there. In fact, some pages take this as far as placing a social media tool bar that scrolls down the page as the user reads. This way, the user always has access to the social media tools offered by the site. Personally, I think this makes sites busier and harder to read. I am not sure if it is a trade off that should be made.

When working at trade shows I often see people holding contests and raffles in exchange for email addresses. These marketing techniques recognize the value of having an instant and free method to contact their users. Unfortunately, this technique is rarely as valuable as it's cracked up to be. It's easily ignored, expensive and time consuming. That is not to say collecting a database of potential and past client emails is not worthwhile. Anyone who has ever leveraged such a collection knows the power of contacting large groups of people without having to address envelopes and lick stamps. But the Open Graph and the connection it forms between the user and the page are far more valuable and are more likely to be viewed by the user. There are two main reasons for this. First, stories are published into the user's feeds in short enough format that even if the user wants to ignore it, chances are by the time they decide to ignore the story they've already read it and it's too late! It's an information blitzkrieg. The second reason the Open Graph is so powerful is that once a user has Liked you, you are able to stay in contact, sending them long form messages– without licking any envelopes. Better still, Their affiliation with you is displayed to their friends. It's like a rotating digital bumper sticker.

Go! Go! Go!

At this point, you should have your Facebook account all set up. You should have the basic information filled out along with links to your other online touch points. Your photo should be up and you should have Liked the page and shamelessly plugged it to all your friends, family and clients. Use your page to become a fan of other local businesses you respect. Interact with them using your page, and most of all, be social! It takes some time to build a following on the world's biggest network, but if you understand the rules laid out above and in the introduction, you should have no problems. Check out the Tools of the Trade in the Twitter section for automation tips and tricks.

You're bringing a lot to the table as it is, but beyond your social skills and enthusiasm, there's one more thing you'll need. To ensure that your social media strategy on Facebook is a success, you'll need persistence. As you're posting, Facebook will be measuring. Use the metrics it generates to see what's working and what isn't. To view your metrics navigate to www.facebook.com/insights, there is even the possibility to link your website to Facebook's insights to measure social interaction. Though, now that google analytics includes this functionality, it may not be worth the effort. Seriously, it's not easy to figure out. Watch your total Likes and interaction rates. Understand what kind of content is receiving the most interaction and don't forget that content timing is important. Good content should produce a spike in both likes and interaction. When you see a spike, take note!

This book can provide a primer on writing content, basic technology and best practices, but everyone's clients are different. Even within an industry, clients are attracted to specific brands for specific reasons. This all goes back to brand strategy (covered in the intro), and it means you need to get creative and create content that appeals to your clients. Never forget that a picture is worth 1000 words. Get yourself a decent digital camera (I like Nikon's d5100 for fool proof, beautiful photos and video, there's a link to it on our site and yes, I will get money if you buy it there). When you create great content, you will attract customers. When you don't, you won't. Bottom line? Always ask yourself, "Is this awesome?"

SECTION IV

TWITTER

Twitter Defined

Twitter is a social networking site that allows two way communication in an immediate and public environment. Imagine a police radio or walkie-talkie chatter, where all communications are broadcast publicly and anyone with a scanner can listen in. Only here, they are all written. Users are able to post 140 character "tweets", which are then syndicated on the home pages of the users who are following the poster. The power of Twitter lies in its users' commitment, assuring constant contact to all of your followers. Your followers will not be reading your subject line and sending the message to the trash, because your subject line is your message. Better yet, the growth of Twitter use on mobile applications has been staggering. More and more people are tweeting on the go. Meaning, if they follow you, you're always with them.

Twitter is a great medium for professionals. It allows us to promote our brand without being promotional, something we should be pros at. Most small businesses are fun, empathetic, engaging or any other anthropomorphic trait you want because small businesses are reflections of their owners. They are all these things while still maintaining professionalism, exactly the kind of company users want to interact with. The average Twitter user is a 30-40 year old professional, mobile, urban and probably a woman, also the demographic for your average social media manager. Twitter can help us build relationships and attract new business from this core group of users.

As Deanna Zandt states in *Share This!*, "The personal is political. Politics is the art and science of changing any kind of power relationship; the cultural norms by which we act." Social media allows insight into the values and interests of our peers that would otherwise be impossible. Imagine trying to impress upon every potential client the depth of your person. A previously crazy notion! But through Twitter, you can build a story of authenticity, personality and depth of character by tweeting about your firm's commitment to the environment, your love of standard poodles or the pride you put into your work. Good luck getting just one of those bullet points out in a face to face sales meeting. Or more likely, on the phone. But, as your clients and potential clients transition to learning about you and connecting with you on social media, the conversation takes place naturally. Your stream will build a narrative over time as you share with your followers. Your stream will create a window onto your brand, which will build authenticity and create a story for your client that is both earnest and condensed. These concepts of earnestness and condensation of thought are what draw users in and why the user will take the time to learn about your brand.

Speaking in Twitter, 101

Before we get started with the nuts and bolts of Twitter, we need to learn some basic lingo. These terms will be explained in depth later when we actually use them, but it's hard to talk about Twitter without talking about tweets, and I don't want to lose anyone.

1) Tweet: a 140 character message broadcast to anyone following the author.
2) Retweet: When a user broadcasts another user's tweet, while attributing it to the author.
3) DM: or, Direct Message. A private message sent from one user to another.
4) Stream: Also called a timeline, it's a complete list of a user's tweets.
5) Replies and Mentions: when one user references another user within a tweet by using an "@".
6) Home Timeline: A collection of all the tweets from users you follow.
7) Hashtags: A "#" is used to denote specific keywords associated with a tweet i.e. #gettingslizzard.

But, Why?

If everyone is already on Facebook, and most users on Twitter are, why bother? I've seen charts that claim only 7% of Twitter users only use Twitter whereas 89% also use Facebook. That number may or may not be accurate, but for our purposes we can assume it is. In fact, let's assume there are no users on Twitter who aren't also on Facebook. So really, why bother? This boils down to one of our basic precepts about social networking: while you may be looking at the exact same set of users, the way they interact with the system and the way the system allows them to interact with one another modifies who you will be connecting with. In simpler terms, Facebook is better for connecting with people. Twitter is better for connecting with businesses. There are three reasons you should be tweeting and they are as follows.

Vendor love

Just like the other tools in the big four have very specific subsets of reasons to use them, Twitter too has a few main draws for the small business. First, "vendor love", aka sucking up, networking, etc. A wedding vendor I once worked for constantly talked about the importance of vendor love. We sent planners we worked with beer and thank you cards while drilling it into our employees' heads that hotel managers were some of our biggest referrers. Did all that work? Of course it did. Was it expensive? Yes. Could it have been accomplished with fewer resources and less time? Absolutely.

Traditional networking tricks (such as swag) can work wonders for getting your brand into your peers' minds. But it's not necessary when the same thing can be accomplished by retweeting some of a photographer's work with some praise. Why? Because a thank you card lets your fellow vendor know you took 10 seconds and 44 cents to thank them. A tweet, even the most mundane, lets your fellow vendor know you enjoyed their thoughts so much as to recommend them to everyone you are connected with on Twitter. This is some seriously low effort with high return on investment.

The retweet, when it comes to vendor love, is the inverse of sending Christmas sausage packages, especially when sending sausage packages to the Jewish wedding planner. She keeps kosher. One of my favorite stories of good intentions gone awry is from that very planner who told me a story of being sent a basket of smoked pork products with a card reading, "Merry X-Mas." Oops. That's part of the beauty of the retweet – you take their words and attribute them to the original vendor. No fuss. No muss. You're not going to offend or misinterpret because you're using their words.

Speaking of vendor love, by retweeting and conversing, you're going to be interacting with your fellow vendors on a regular basis. This keeps you at the front of their minds. If you're a tiler and I'm a cabinet maker meeting with a couple that wants a backsplash, you can bet your name will be coming up in my sales meeting.

Web traffic

A second reason, and an important one, is SEO, or search engine optimization. Google officially recognizes Twitter in its search algorithm. That means that by engaging with others on Twitter you are boosting your website in search engine results. Your direct competitor may have a much bigger online media budget than you, but it may not engage in quality social media strategy and management. If that's the case you're gonna crush them. Being on

Twitter also gives you the opportunity to make it easier for others to link to you. It lowers the barriers for someone to link to you if you've done all the work for them and they can just retweet your thoughts with one mouse click. The more links to your website out there, the higher your website shows up in search engine rankings.

Your clients expect it

Do it for your clients! The third reason may seem superfluous since all our hypothetical twitterers are also on Facebook, but you can bet that if they are on both, they want to see you on both. This is especially important for the smaller companies out there that don't rely on office visits to make sales. Like we talked about in the intro, your social media outlets are your storefront; having a strong, quality presence on them equates to an impressive and well furnished showroom. However, that's not to say there are no new clients to be had on Twitter. Business to business clients are out there. If you are B2B or want to be, Twitter is your medium.

Some brands use Twitter for customer service. This may work well for them, but I think it is just a ploy for social media managers to make tangible work for themselves so they have something to present to upper management. If you're in an organization where you need to show such results on a short timeline, I say go for it. If you're not, save yourself the headache. You are already spending enough time on email. A company I worked for sometimes had people asking for quotes via Twitter. Not something I would ever do, but people are engaging companies in these new media and you need to be able to engage them back. If someone does take the time to ask you for a quote on Twitter, take the time to answer, but do it privately or refer them to your email publicly to signal to others that you won't field such questions publicly. If someone asks a question you commonly answer on the phone, by all means answer it on Twitter. That's great content. It's informative, casual and conversational. Bonus points if you can answer while being funny.

The take away here is that Twitter is an important tool and you should be using it, but I wouldn't expect to see too many clients directly engaging you from it. There are friendlier, easier ways to interact with your clients, and they will choose those paths. Instead, we are going to concentrate on some methods for creating a presence that will allow you to effectively network with your industry peers while boosting your search engine rankings.

I might not get overly excited when I talk about the importance of Twitter or its abilities, but I love it. I really do. Here's why – it's simple. You can change your background and your photo, but everything else is text. It lets the message shine, and it doesn't complicate the message with complex rules about what messages will be displayed to whom. Technically, it's easier to explain, and it doesn't take much maintenance. I'm a big fan of simple, and I believe most Internet users are as well. It comes back to that short attention span. Twitter is great at getting your message out there in an effective manner without a bunch of fluff to distract users. I believe that extra fluff is what killed MySpace and also why companies are having such a hard time monetizing Facebook – there are just too many places for your attention to go!

Getting Started

Sign up. You'll need a unique user name, hopefully your business name isn't taken, but it's a big world with many, many users. You have fifteen characters total, which should be plenty with a little creativity. If your business name is taken attempt to shorten it and add the city. For example:

GreatEvents- taken
GreatEventsMN- Taken
GreatEventsMSP Open
GreatEventsMPLS Open
YourGreatEvents Open

There are ways to find a unique user ID that pertains to you. In this case, you might even be able to take some action if you've trademarked your name and someone else is using it, especially if they aren't using the account. Twitter calls this "name squatting", and it's against its terms of service. If you have a trademarked name and someone is (or isn't) tweeting with it, you can go get it.[11] This is another example of Twitter's business friendliness.

As a basic rule, you want your name to be as short as possible. This makes it easier for people to reference you in their tweets. If that doesn't make sense now, it will soon. You'll also want

---

[11]For more information on name squatting visit Twitter's help center here: http://support.twitter.com/groups/33-report-a-violation/topics/148-policy-information/articles/18370-name-squatting-policy

your name to be easy to say and easy to remember. Avoid the trap of underscores, hyphens and substituting numbers for letters or sections of words. Imagine trying to give someone your user name over the phone if it is @h8_no1. Just because it made a great license plate doesn't mean it's going to make a great twitter name. The same rules apply to buying a domain name for your website: short, simple and easy to say. (Be sure to make a good password! See the intro for a primer on the subject.)

You'll also choose your name when signing up. This name is different than your unique user name that we just talked about above. It does not need to be unique, and you'll have 20 characters in which to place your business name. If your business name is more than 20 characters and you don't have anything shorter to go by, you're going to have to get creative again.

When you choose a user ID it's important to like it and know that it will be your name for a while, or forever. While you can change your Twitter handle later and keep all your current followers, old tweets that mention you will not be updated, and all those links will become broken. If a user is blown away by a great comment someone else made about you and they used your old name, the user might try and find you using the old name. They will then either find a blank page or, worse, someone else's page. *No beuno*.

Once you have a great name, your next step will be to customize your account. It's very, very important to have an avatar. An avatar is a user's visual representation of him or herself. It's your profile picture, but we use the word avatar because it could be a drawing or a graphic or a letter or etc. There is much debate on what exactly makes the best avatar, but cutting through the static, we find there are basically two acceptable choices. You should choose either a photo of yourself or your logo. The way you use your account is what dictates the type of avatar you should use. Will it just be one person tweeting or a team?

If you have a company with more than a few people and you'll have more than a few people tweeting, your logo will work for your profile picture. However, in that case you should consider giving everyone who will be tweeting their own account. This will allow users to build that personal relationship they are looking for with your brand, something not as easily achieved with a logo when compared to a face. These accounts then should follow the same rules as if it was just you tweeting and should have a photo as their profile picture. Sounds like it's going to be collectively more work, doesn't it? It will be.

Realistically, in a small operation (less than 50 employees and one geographic territory) there is no need to have more than one or two people running the show. To think that more than just a few people will be able to sustain the interest to build an account is wishful thinking anyways. Tweeting may look like fun from the outside, but it really is hard work. If it's just going to be a few people tweeting, I suggest getting a group shot for your avatar. Photo booths work wonders for this. If it's just one person, go for the head shot.

In most cases, you want a photograph to be your profile picture. This goes a long way to make your brand more personable as well as building your credibility. It's easier to trust a person with a photograph and a real name when you're viewing them online, and it helps build the authenticity. Since trust and authenticity are what we are going for, I highly recommend the photo.

If you aren't yet sure if you will be group tweeting or tweeting solo, start as a group with your logo. In all likelyhood, after a few weeks the group will weed itself out and you'll be left with the individual(s) who will actually be doing the work and you can decide from there whether it's best to have one account or multiple accounts and what kind of avatar to use.

Your bio is next, and it has to be brief. Try and capture the feel of your brand in just a few sentences. It's tough. The Traveling

Photo Booth's Los Angeles branch did a great job of this when it tweeted:

"Tweeting from the best photo booth in the galaxy! Spreading the photo booth love to our fellow Angelenos."

    The tweet managed to explain what the company does in real life, what it will be doing on Twitter, established dominance and reinforced brand identity in just two sentences. It does all that with a sense of humor and manages to be personable at the same time. There is a tendency to gloss over the bio section, but it is worth putting the effort into.

    There are two more things to cover for the basic user, but there will be an advanced section to follow if you are looking at getting more in depth. The link to your website is also very important, be sure to include it. That goes back to our policy of always making it easy for the user to move between media. Then there is the background and design. If you have an image you can pull from some advertising work or a texture you use on your collateral, go ahead and use it. If you're not sure how it's going to look or you're slapping something up just to have a custom background, stop. The old adage about the chain only being as strong as its weakest link applies here. A poorly designed background is bad for credibility. It takes away from all your hard work elsewhere. If you aren't sure about a background, just stick with the default choices Twitter offers. No one will judge you for it. That is especially true since more and more people are accessing Twitter from outside applications like TweetDeck or from their phone. That demographic continues to grow, and many people won't ever see your background because of it.

Advanced account issues

The link to your website: There are two major things to consider if you have the capability to link to your website, analytics and entry points. If you're using some analytics or tracking software for your website, you can track the Twitter link as the entry to your site. Why is this important? Twitter's analytic back end isn't yet very strong. The hope here is that people will follow the link to your site after viewing something interesting on Twitter. This certainly won't give you the complete picture, but it's going to help. One way to accomplish this is by having a separate landing page for links from Twitter, like www.cloutsmiths.com/twitter/.

Your background: If you have a graphic designer or are yourself talented in the art form, there are a few things to consider when building a background. First, size. We know the average user has a screen resolution of 1024x768, so this is the size I would use to begin designing. The main Twitter feed area is 760 pixels wide and will be centered, so the space on the left is available for all kinds of information or images. I don't like filling this space with info about your Facebook page, your email, etc. It gets busy very fast, and it's frustrating to see data that isn't clickable when you know it should be. It should all be on your website anyways. Also, since you are designing your image to be 1024 pixels wide, anything larger than that will have blank space to the right of your background. Therefore, you should incorporate into the right edge of your background a solid color so the transition from your background image to the blank space looks seamless.

How to Build a Following

Now that you are set up with a fully functioning and attractive Twitter account, you're ready to go! Well not yet, I first want you to set up a second account. We're going to use this as a throw away account. This account will be used to see who's worth following without first following them on your business account. It's going to allow you meet people, without blowing your only chance at the first impression, and it's going to allow you to be a silent observer. This is an account you should plan on tossing once your observation period is over, so it can be an existing personal account or the account you made for your business last year and left for dead because it was boring. If you are using an existing account, especially one associated with your business, change the user ID, name and bio info. You don't want the account to be identified as yours. Scratch off the VIN numbers. You're going to ride that account to the border and abandon it for dead when you hit Mexico. It's time for a fresh start.

Even if you don't go out, find a few local twitterers who do and follow them on your throw away account. All major cities have at least one free weekly paper. In Minneapolis it's the *City Pages*, Milwaukee's is *The Shephard Express*, NYC has the *Village Voice* and Portland *The Mercury*. Find yours and use it to your benefit by following them on your throw away account. Next, find 30 or so companies that you already work with, anticipate working with or want to work with. Find businesses you like: venues, restaurants, coffee shops, bars you like to go to, etc. Most cities have a local chain of hip restaurants that everyone knows about. They are also probably tweeting. Try and find that restaurant group and see who they are following. It will be a great start, and I'm guessing you will find all kinds of people working in your industry to connect with you didn't even know existed. This part is like attending an industry get together, only everyone is wearing name tags, being candid and not drunk.

Okay, why the hell am I following all these people and not writing anything myself? The goal for your first two weeks is to populate a good stream. You want to have interesting content before you start following anyone. Once you have a good stream going on your real account it's time to start following people there. The reason you are waiting to follow people is because they are more likely to follow you back if you actually have a solid stream. A user is most likely to follow you when they are notified that you are starting to follow them. If you don't yet have any tweets and you start to follow people, they get that notification, they will look at your account, see it's empty and they won't follow you back. Why would they? You haven't said anything! Then you just fade away in their memory and it's harder to get them to follow you, retweets be damned.

A note on personal Twitter accounts

For small business owners on Twitter, trash your personal account. Concentrate on your work account. I don't feel that having a personal Twitter is necessary. First, after a spending all day with TweetDeck open on my work computer, the last thing I want to do when I get home is fire off some personal tweets. Really, do you come home and want to fire up Quicken? Didn't think so.

Second, though you may not mention that you are explicitly affiliated with a company, as long as you are a figurehead you will be inexorable from that company. We all do industry events. They are important (as much as we sometimes wish they weren't), so people know your name, they know what you look like and they might even know you have a Twitter account. This is especially important for those who use their name in their brand! Don't think Google isn't going to pull up your Twitter stream just because your client searched for Dingbat Engineering instead of Leslie Dingbat. In fact, I'd wager that dear Leslie's Twitter account shows up above her engineering business.

If you are so compelled to maintain both a personal and a work Twitter account, keep the following in mind:

Just as you should moderate your Twitter stream to avoid mentioning religion or politics for your business, you should moderate your personal stream. As mentioned before, if you are a figurehead at your business and other people know your name, your streams are bound to be intermingled. Case in point, I follow a certain bakery – they make amazing cakes and I was very impressed with some of the philanthropic work they do. I also like cake. I often engaged them and helped promote their brand via my Twitter stream. I'd retweet news for them, share their events, etc. However, I was also following one of the owners' personal account on Twitter. At first she wasn't a heavy user and there was an occasional generic tweet. Then, she got hooked. Tweets were coming out hourly on bad days and every 20 minutes on good days, or was it the other way around? There was a shift in content over time. The owner began to treat her account as her soap box. The occasional bland tweet transformed into a nonstop feed of vitriol, religion and politics. This may seem like a farfetched example, but think about the way you talk with your friends and the way you talk at an association meeting. Would you ever dream of telling a fellow vendor who you voted for? Telling them your views on unions? Quoting the Bible to them? Well, yeah okay. I've had a few too many and gone a little too far with fellow vendors – which reminds me, don't tweet drunk. These are all things that are fine in private, and in 140 characters may seem too short to matter, but they are also too short to have any finesse. Something you find funny may come off as seriously antagonistic to others.

If you absolutely insist on being an ass online, fine, but set your Twitter account to private, use a fake name and don't let anyone friend you. Or, keep a diary so everyone can see what a jerk you were after you die instead of right now.

I've included this note specifically here because on Facebook we can make the privacy settings a little more fine grained, but I'd still suggest a heavy dose of moderation, even if your privacy settings make the iron curtain look open.

The first tweet

It's time for your first official tweet as a business. Tweet to yourself. It may seem crazy to talk to yourself, but it's good practice and it builds credibility for when you go "live." It's a chance to fill up your stream with quality content so when others get notice that you've started to follow them, they will follow you back. Read what the people you followed on your throw away are saying. If anyone says anything interesting or funny, retweet it on your real account like this *RT @AwesomeBar (the original tweet)*.

Retweeting is like saying ditto but with attribution. The RT shows that it was a retweet, the @AwesomeBar shows who the original author was and that's all followed by the original content. People love to get retweeted because it means you think their content had value, so much value that you wanted to share it with your followers. It's just a nice thing to do. It also looks good on your stream since you're posting all kinds of good content. See an interesting fact about the tall ship convention in town? Retweet it. You can also paraphrase and rephrase. If the local weekly is organizing a pub crawl, you could write, "Wow! @LocalWeekly has a pub crawl that looks awesome!" This is called a "mention" and people love to be mentioned, especially when it's unsolicited. Here again, attribution is key. Your comment will also show up in their stream on Twitter, a great way for new users to find you. All this will build credibility, will make users feel good about working with you since you're a local and will allow them to connect with you. This is what the great Kurt Vonnegut called a Granfalloon or "a proud and meaningless association of human beings." Self-help books call this human connection. I call it an ice breaker and a valuable sales tool.

Retweeting is a great example of something called a gift economy. As Wikipedia defines it, a gift economy is, "A society where valuable goods and services are regularly given without any explicit agreement for immediate or future rewards (i.e. no formal *quid pro quo* exists)." Conveniently, another example of a gift economy is Wikipedia itself. The site is composed entirely of articles written and edited by users who receive no compensation. By recognizing this, we can see why a retweet is useful beyond the immediate gratitude felt by the original author or the retweet's ability to plant your brand in the back of their mind. Marcel Mauss, the famed sociologist, recognized that gifts come with implicit obligation. Last Christmas my upstairs neighbors baked me cookies without prompting. A lovely gesture, but unfortunately I was on a diet. (And also terrified of razor blades hidden in tasty goodies. Damn after school specials making me paranoid!) So the cookies went on to be digested by seagulls. Even though I didn't want the cookies and I didn't eat the cookies, I felt obligated to return the favor to my upstairs neighbor with my own baked goods. In turn, I will be obligated to continue this tradition until I die from eating a razor-bladed cupcake, or I move out. It's also fairly common to have an aunt with whom this phenomena exists. Search your family tree and you will no doubt begin to form a deep, personal understanding of the gift economy and its implicit obligations. You will also understand the power of the retweet, which is just a nice little gift that doesn't require baking.

Along with retweeting and mentioning, you will want to build your own content. The first rule is to be personal. That's what this is all about, and it's why you are getting your own Twitter account. Is there something cool going on at the bar down the street?

Tweet about it. Is your company going to be at a trade show? Sponsoring a 5k? Tweet about it. Did the UPS guy track dog crap into your office? Tweet about it. Doing Twitter right means sharing valuable information, asking valid questions or triggering good conversations, just like every other medium. Only on Twitter, we don't have as much fluff to hide behind if we can't be engaging. It also means being a local business people can identify with.

After you have enough tweets (aim for 40) only then should you start following people. Spread all that out over a week or two. Don't burn yourself out. This way, when you follow your first people, which should be fellow small businesses, they will look at your stream and see that you have quality content (instead of nothing) and will be more likely to follow you back. Hopefully at this point some of the people you've mentioned or retweeted have already started to follow you and you're on your way to a long and happy relationship with the Twitter community.

At this point, you should pretty much have a knack for it. There are some tools we can use to extend our skills and reflect upon the content we generate and how effective it is, but because all messages are displayed to all followers, it's hard to know if your tweet actually made an impression on them unless they take the time to react to it. Of course, if your followers do take the time to react to something, take note! That's a great tweet (unless someone was compelled to tell you how much they hated it). It's also good practice when someone does take the time to reply to you or retweet that you not to let the ball drop. This is a conversation, and it's rude to ignore someone who's talking to you.

Finding people to follow (and thusly people to follow you) is not 100% straight forward. There are some advanced tools out there like ChirpCity and Twiangulate that can help you find followers in your area or niche, but the first step, like in so many other areas, is to pause. Think about who you should follow and why you should follow them. Bear in mind when following people that there is no real benefit to following everyone and anyone. Instead, you should focus on peers you already know and respect, people who might be able to help your business and even tangentially related companies. While those advanced tools mentioned above can be helpful, Twitter has its own search version with some nifty tools that can be much easier to use and return high quality results on its own. Looking for keywords like your city name and product offering can help you find people in the know and point you in the right direction.

Lists can also be helpful for finding people to follow once you have already located a few peers. Lists are just what the name implies. A list of users that has been grouped by category by a user, you can even make your own list. The benefit to tagging all the people you follow with a category is to build authority on a subject. If you build high quality lists, you are essentially building authority by association. A final native tool to Twitter, and the tool I use most to find people to follow, is Twitter Recommends. I like it because the tool already knows what industry I'm in by the people I follow and where I am and can recommend other users based on those traits. It's six degrees of separation, but with a way to build a connection in real time. Another small benefit is how the tool only recommends a few people at a time so it's harder to go on follow binges, which always leave you feeling dirty in the morning.

Lists are similarly important if you have multiple accounts for one company. Each Twitter member should have a list that contains all the other accounts for the company. It's frustrating for a user to come across your brand's help desk when they are looking for the marketing department. Give them the directions they need to get to the right place.

Speaking of follow binges, be sure to follow people who play by the same rules as you. Avoid chronic overposters, the boring and those who refuse to engage in conversation. They aren't going to do you any good, and they are going to take your attention away from the people who are actually engaging in conversation with you.

It's worth mentioning here Twitter memes. These are horrible rotten things that Twitter users insist on doing, even though they do little if anything to improve your standing on Twitter. You will see, at some point, these hashtags "#FF" or "#WW." Respectively they mean Follow Friday and Wedding Wednesday (or, if you're not a wedding vendor- Wine Wednesday.) Either way, they were originally created as a way to promote Twitter feeds that the tweeter thinks are worth following. They rapidly devolved into long lists of user names with no discussion on what or why the people included on the list should be followed. If you insist on taking part in this meme, make it look like this:

@TheCloutSmiths is an awesome resource for social media tips and tricks! #FF

> NOT

@TheCloutSmiths @TwitterHandle @AnotherPerson @NeverEnding @StringOfNonsense @ThatIsJustAnnoying #FF

See the difference? Of course you do.

Best Practices

Protected accounts

Twitter offers you the possibility of having a "protected account." In short, this means that only those users you approve can see your feed. This is not going to be a good idea for your business account. The problem, besides hiding all your content from interested users, is that users will not be able to retweet your content. This seriously hinders the ability to grow your network in a truly viral sense.

O RLY?

Professionalism is as important here as it is in any other printed material your brand may circulate. I've seen people trying to get around Twitter's brevity rule with text messaging grammar that even the most text happy 14 year old girl would have trouble deciphering. "UR" stands for "you are" and it makes anyone looking at it think UR a moron. Let's imagine for a minute that we are in some ideal world where you could conduct an exit interview with every lost sale. In conducting your interview, your client may not be able to articulate why they were turned off by your stream, but if you're abbreviating "to" or "too" with 2 (Two is acceptable to abbreviate in this fashion.) it probably has something to do with it. Also, emoticons have no place in the business world. Use your words. Oh really? Yes. Really.

Broken attribution

Make sure that when you are retweeting something the original user gets credit for it. Don't copy and paste the message without their name. It's rude. As you have or will find, people work hard for their content and want credit. Also, if someone posts a shortened URL from a different service and you are going to tweet about it yourself after hearing about it from them – but not a retweet – use their shortened link instead of your own. This is a courtesy and it helps the original user track the spread of their link.

Protecting your tweets

In a similar vein, allow room for retweets to make sure you get attribution for your content. If your user name is "hambone" and your tweets are awesome, people will want to retweet you (our goal). But keep in mind that people won't be able to retweet your entire post if you use all 140 characters because they will need to add "RT @hambone," 11 extra characters. Instead they will only be able to retweet 129 characters. So, if you can manage to keep your posts below 129 characters that's all the better. It won't always be possible, but it reduces the chances of your attribution being dropped so the retweeter doesn't have to edit the content of your message.

Address your addressee

Referring to someone by their real name when they have an account is like talking about someone at your dinner table in the third person. They are right there and you should engage them. So, Bar La Grassa becomes @barlagrassa. That way, my followers know that Bar La Grassa is on Twitter and have an easy way to connect with them. Also, Bar La Grassa gets notified that I was talking about them. These are two very valuable opportunities for advanced connection that would otherwise be missed by typing in the full proper name of one of the best restaurants in the Twin Cities. (I hope they read this book and hook me up.)

Also, where you mention your addressee matters! Unless the reader is following both you and TheDude, if you write, "@TheDude That rug really tied the room together, man," it will not show up in your stream because Twitter thinks you intended the message to be a reply to part of a conversation. Instead you can write, ".@TheDude My condolences for the loss of Donny." The period moves the @ away from the first character, tricking Twitter into thinking you meant the message for everyone. Another way to do it is to just write the message with the mention at the end or in line.

Overly promotional RTs

The retweet is great for many reasons, and it can be a great way to expand your following and credibility. They can also be really annoying to your users. Retweeting useful information is great. Retweeting every time anyone mentions you is annoying. Can you imagine if someone in real life said to you every day, "You will never believe how great Tina said I am!" "Bill thinks I'm the best!" Or, "James thinks we are great!" Once in a while is fine, but do it with a sense of humility. Or better, spin the message while remembering the tips for addressing the addressee. Those posts are wonderful and your users aren't going to see them, but you can make them see something like this:

"Thanks for the kind words @YourFan! We try our best to have great service. It's nice to hear it's working!"

You can get the point across without being a braggart. You thank the user directly and you still give them the benefit of retweeting – all without sounding like a smug jerk.

Down with Foursquare!

"But I thought you liked Foursquare?!" I do, but not when it's on Twitter (or Facebook). Please don't cross populate. In the global rules section, we talked about why not to do this between Twitter and Facebook, but there are so many more reasons to not do this between so many other sources. I have a good friend whom I no longer communicate with on Twitter or Facebook because he is an avid user of Foursquare. You may know the type. Every day this friend goes to the same coffee shop to get his morning latte, to the same grocery every Wednesday and the same bars every weekend. He's also a mobile worker, so when he's not at his normal coffee shop, he's checking in somewhere else, usually a coffee shop.

Every morning when I open up my Twitter stream and my Facebook account, I know he's had his morning coffee. I know when he's hungry, where he eats and when he goes to buy stamps. I can expect half a dozen updates a day from him, and they are pretty much the same every day. I don't care where you are, Danny. I really don't. I told you on Twitter and I called you to tell you how damned annoying it is and now it's going in my book. You annoyed me that much with your checking in. If someone wants to know where you are and you want people to be able to find out such information (Maybe because you're worried you're being followed by a stealthy assassin and leaving a trail for the police?), let them log into Foursquare or Yelp to find out. Save Twitter for when your morning latte is particularly amazing because the barista put her number in the foam, or when you spill said latte in your lap while checking in on Foursquare. Remember the power of self deprecating humor.

A caveat: my pox upon cross population doesn't apply to YouTube videos or sites that host actual content that isn't otherwise easily searchable or identifiable to your brand. Posting a link to a video you made and hosted on YouTube is, in fact, encouraged.

Shutup! Shutup! Shutup!

Don't broadcast too frequently. Broadcasting on Twitter is posting content that is not conversational. People may get bored or annoyed, especially if your content seems at all self promotional or anything like advertising. Don't be a robot. It also won't do much to earn you new followers.

Auto reply is the devil

Don't fall into the trap of thinking that everyone who follows you wants an instant message thanking them for the follow. It's silly, and no one cares. Sending a form message assures the new follower, beyond a shadow of a doubt, that you don't care that they followed you. It's better to leave them guessing than to prove them right. Instead, just follow them right back without saying anything. You can use an auto follower if you insist, but I prefer to actually look at each individual follower's profile to make sure they are real. Interestingly, the quality of the users you follow reflects upon you in search engine rankings. Yup, it's more complicated than a credit score and it might be more important. Weird. Really though, the volume for a local business isn't going to be large enough that you cannot handle all this by hand. Set up a filter using your email software/website that will put all email from Twitter into a folder, and check that folder once a week. It's better to make a user wait a week before you follow them back than following them back instantly. It's yet another way to build authenticity and show there is a real person toiling away behind that computer screen.

A Case Study

Twitter is a place where relationships can start with one mouse click and can end just as easily. It's because of this we can get some very heavy hitters to tacitly endorse us, even if we have never met or spoken to them before. For example, at a company I tweeted for I had within one week a Project Runway contestant, an American Idol contestant and Backcountry.com tweeting while referencing my brand. How? I sent them goofy messages. The Backcountry.com story is my favorite because I killed a whole telephone line full of birds with one stone.

Large brands like Backcountry.com are great targets for building your clout and gaining followers. Because they usually employ full time social media managers, there is going to be someone there who has the specific job of reading your tweet and replying to it. They are also likely to have a huge number of followers. Backcountry.com has 9,000 followers on Twitter and 200,000 on Facebook. You can bet that stream gets a lot of eyeballs on it. So when a huge brand like that tweets about you, that's 17,991 eyeballs, or 9,000 followers x 1.999 eyeballs per person (not everyone has both eyeballs), that your Twitter handle will come in front of. Each set of eyeballs will come away with the impression that Backcountry.com, a brand they love, endorses you. Expect quite a few followers to come out of something like that. But wait, there's more!

Remember that we are in a gift economy. What if you could take a vendor you are friends with and give them a little boost using our technique to manipulate the streams of huge corporations? Well your vendor friend would owe you. Big time. (Or in a more Midwestern sensibility, they would really appreciate your efforts, and what goes around comes around. Don't cha' know.) A photographer did a photo shoot in Minnesota where the bride and groom were standing on the end of a pier, in January. Cold. The bride wore a white Marmot jacket and the groom wore a black Patagonia jacket with black pants and huge boots. I thought it was a great photo that captured the bride and groom's sensibilities and personalities, but it also captured the brand names of two very large outdoor brands. I tweeted appropriately:

@backcountrycom @photographernameremoved this should be a new marmot advertisement. http://bit.ly/shortlink

Oh yes, this was retweeted by Backcountry.com. Our brand was shown to all those eyeballs and I was thanked profusely by said photographer, who from then on paid very special attention to my stream.

Dell has 1.5 million followers. Do you have a vendor friend who just bought a new computer? Is it a Dell? Try:

I'm so jealous of @vendorfriend and their new @DellHomeus computer, maybe if I had one I could get more work done (hint hint boss?)

It may or may not be retweeted by Dell, but you've mentioned your vendor friend, which they will undoubtedly appreciate. You've also tweeted some decent content. Is this tweet relevant to anyone but you? No, not really. But it does reinforce that you are a person. It's humorous because everyone can relate to wanting a new computer, and it will keep your followers listening to you.

Magazines are a great resource for the twitterer to increase their reach easily. As large brands, they usually have large following and have specific strategies that can be taken advantage of. Vogue has become well known for retweeting questions that stump their team. This has two main advantages for them: first, it improves loyalty of the user they interact with, and second, it shows they are willing to look for information they may not have, increasing their level of authority. For the same reasons, this is a great strategy to implement yourself. This is all beneficial for you, since if you can stump the Vogue Twitter team, your tweet can be sent out to all of their 165,000 followers.

You can also try for celebrities, but bear in mind they are less likely to respond since they may not have someone dealing with their Twitter for them and they are more likely to have people mentioning them constantly. That means they have to sift through a lot of noise to find your tweet at them. You might get lucky, and a celebrity endorsement is never bad. Go for it, but it's not going to be as easy as getting an airline or a large retailer to mention you. I get the impression that those social media managers are bored stiff and are just waiting for interaction, any interaction.

The Tool Box

TweetDeck: An amazing application that can streamline your tweeting and supercharge your work flow. Best of all, it's free and it works on pretty much every device out there. TweetDeck is what allowed me to use Twitter less than 20 minutes a week and build a stellar stream that attracted a great deal of followers. This was made possible in so little time by taking advantage of scheduling. With TweetDeck you can sign into both your Twitter and Facebook account and schedule all your updates and tweets for as far in advance as you can manage to think. I like to work in quarterly increments. For instance, in December I scheduled tweets for Valentine's Day, New Year's Day, two contests, tips that would be broadcast every Tuesday, jokes, thank-yous for friendly vendors for their help with our Halloween party and announcements for upcoming events. One tweet a day for 2.5 months. It took about four hours to come up with all that, but I wouldn't have to look at it again until March. Whenever something new came up such as a trade show or a new business development, I'd add it to my scheduled tweets and presto, I had designed a dynamic Twitter stream that was as hands off as possible.

TweetDeck is also great for keeping all the info that will be pouring in organized. It will help you keep track of tweets that mention you and direct messages. It's a better system than relying on the emails Twitter sends out when one of those actions are performed. Just a disclaimer, TweetDeck will only work while it is open. TweetDeck also allows the posting of images and auto shortening of links using the services of your choice. This can be set in preferences along with a slew of other options you should investigate for yourself. All this functionality is also available for Facebook, Foursquare, LinkedIn, GoogleBuzz and MySpace.

Bonus Tip: Since you can schedule your tweets down to the minute with TweetDeck, it makes sense to send them when they are most likely to be read. There are three times typically identified when activity is highest, around lunch between 11 a.m. and noon and also when everyone's brains are fried and they are waiting for the clock to run out, 4:00 p.m. These are also great times for you to hop on and reply and retweet. Aim for 2-4 of these a day. It shouldn't take more than 5 minutes to hammer them out. Skim the people you follow, and when you happen upon something remotely interesting click the retweet button on TweetDeck and you're set. If you come across a bunch, click the retweet button and schedule them out so you can skip it tomorrow.

Of course, tweeting during peak times also means your content has more competition. Hopefully your tweets are compelling enough that they will stand out, but there is something to be said for tweeting during off times. This also applies to posting on Facebook. Posting during lulls means your content is more likely to be read by power users, or users that are always on. These are also the people who will be most likely to share your content as influencers. There is no easy answer for which method is better and again, it depends on who you are looking to attract. Try them both. See what happens.

HootSuite: This is similar in functionality to TweetDeck, but takes advantage of "the cloud." That means HootSuite and all the information you store and access on it is actually stored online instead of on your computer. It also means you can schedule out updates and not worry about your computer being on or a program being open to send them out. The analytics available on HootSuite are also great, but you do have to pay for them. You also have to pay if you want more than one user to be able to log into the accounts associated with your business. The difference in cost is why I can't recommend HootSuite hands down over TweetDeck. Also, I just don't think it's as pretty. However, if you are highly mobile and would like to schedule updates from anywhere, from any computer, or you don't want to leave your computer on all the time, HootSuite is definitely the way to go.

Bitly: Signing up for Bitly from its website will give you link shortening functionality and some tools to measure trends from your tweets. After you sign up, you can set TweetDeck to automatically shorten links using Bitly and attach them to your account with the use of the Bitly API (found under settings on Bitly and services in preferences for TweetDeck). Bitly then gives you access to its statistics page by just adding a + to the end of the shortened URL. So, http://bit.ly/gSwLhL becomes http://bit.ly/gSwLhL+. You then get access to all kinds of great data to help you track your successes in tweeting.

Plixi: Plixi allows you to upload photos and provides you with a shortened url to view them. I choose to use it because it works with TweetDeck and the application I use to tweet on my phone, EchoFon. It also provides plenty of data about your links such as views and retweets associated with the link.

Twitalyzer: The analytics that Twitter didn't come with are offered by Twitalyzer. This service will break your account into five categories that are scored based on their algorithm. The categories are:
Influence: Your impact upon your network.
Signal to Noise: A measure of quality over quantity as measured by people's interactions with your tweets.

Generosity: How much you are sharing the content of others. This term makes perfect sense since we are thinking about Twitter as a gift economy.

Velocity: How often you tweet. Of course this factors into all the other categories.

Clout: Do people reference you? Are you trusted? Do you have Twitter cred? This numbers reveal all.

These concepts should all seem familiar, since these are all essentially measures of our goals on Twitter. By assigning them numbers you should be able to gauge how successfully you are accomplishing your goals and tweak your efforts accordingly. For example, if your influence or clout is low, people aren't interacting with your posts. If your generosity is low, stop being a scrooge and start retweeting. However, don't let one low score spook you if everything else is high, and don't let all low scores spook you. Read about them, how they are measured and remember that you are a small business owner and will never have the same clout as @AndersonCooper.

There are countless applications like Twitalyzer out there. I prefer Twitalyzer because I think the way it breaks down its metrics is most valuable. It's also free. www.Klout.com offers another nice analytics platform, as does TweetStats. Twitter also has their own platform, but as of now the tool is only available to advertisers on Twitter, who can "promote" trends (a promoted hashtag), tweets or accounts. Currently, advertising is too expensive to be worth considering when Google Adwords and Facebook Ads are currently much cheaper and have proven ROI. I don't doubt this will change soon.

Mobility: Morgan Stanley predicts that within the next two years, smart phone shipments will outpace computer sales. The

Japanese version of Facebook now is viewed more than 80% of the time on a mobile phone. So if you don't have a smart phone, it's probably time to jump on the bandwagon. The best part about using a mobile phone is the ability to snap a picture and share it across your media. If you do have a smart phone, great! Download an application to allow you to interact with Twitter. I can't recommend an app here for every phone out there because the list is constantly changing, and I haven't used them all. Your best bet will be to go to Google and search: "Your smart phone, free Twitter app." You'll get plenty of results. One thing to bear in mind is to make sure the app you choose supports both Bitly and Plixi, or a different photo sharing utility of your choice that is also used by TweetDeck or HootSuite. It's best to keep all your services the same across platforms.

SECTION V

MOBILE APPLICATIONS

Mobile Enabled Applications

If you're already on Yelp or Foursquare or know a fair amount about either, you might be wondering, "Why are these lumped together here?" Mobility. Both of these applications, and many more, interface with the GPS abilities of the newest generations of smart phones. With this technology, location based services can offer the user loyalty rewards, coupons and other hyper local promotions. Compared to Facebook or Twitter, these are the new kids on the block and represent the possibility for truly disruptive applications. Every day, exciting new ways to take advantage of location based applications are launched. One such program, TopGuest, allows me to check in at hotels for hotel points, Yelp check-ins allow me to announce that I'm at a restaurant in exchange for elite status on their network.

Foursquare is an application that allows a user to check into places using their phone in exchange for recognition as a regular, access to promotions and "badges." Local businesses develop and offer these promotions, and the user checks in to get access to the promotion. Foursquare is interesting because it has opened up its network to developers, and there are countless add-ons and versions of the program.

Yelp combines the benefits of the mobile check-in with its expansive collection of user rated reviews. This section focuses on Yelp because its features are richer and the addition of reviews makes it more important for a social media manager to watch. While Foursquare absolutely has its merits and I am a member at both and would encourage you to explore both, talking about Yelp's check-in feature can essentially be interchangeable with discussion of Foursquare's application, the same can be said of Facebook's Places.

There aren't any instructions on setting up the various accounts here, the sites are all self explanatory. To succeed on Yelp, Foursquare or Facebook Places just remember these few simple tips.

1. KISS or Keep it simple stupid. Avoid complicated specials. It's tempting to require users to jump through hoops to get specials but it's a turn off for customers and extra work for staff. Keeping it simple ensures users will want to take advantage of the offer and staff excitement.

2. Speaking of staff, make sure they know how to recognize, promote and ring up the specials! This is made much easier by offering the same promotion across platforms.

3. Giving away the house. People respond to fairly minor incentives on mobile check-in driven apps. Don't over do it. Something as simple as 10% off one item on first visit can be plenty to get users to check in.

Why Should I Start Using Yelp?

The first reason, and the hardest to argue against, is that you are already on it. Second, chances are, your customers have already been reviewing you. Yelp has quickly become one of the largest and most trusted user review sites on the Internet. Their mix of humor, innovation, sponsored parties and real life interaction make the service a favorite for users and engenders die hard yelpers. Yelp, thanks to its users, is a phenomenal tool that has changed the way I travel. It has guided me to some of the best restaurants I've ever been to, restaurants that in many cases would have been impossible to find on my own. Many of the top travel shows admit to using Yelp extensively during their research process, and it makes perfect sense. I feel bad for all the would-be interns out there who will never get a research position on The Travel Channel because of Yelp. Yelp has, until March of 2011, been only in North America. As someone with a diagnosed case of wanderlust, I'm very excited to report that Yelp is now rolling out in Europe. Smörgåsbord, anyone?

Yelp has also changed the way we shop. Sixty-three percent of shoppers read reviews online before they make any shopping decisions. That means I'm not going to call you, email you or walk out my door until my purchasing decision has been made with information I have found from sources other than you and your sales clerks. That can be great news, if you are managing your reviews properly. It's even better news since reviews on a site can boost conversion rates by 20%. An informed client is an easier sell when you have a great product and they know it.

To get started on Yelp, the business owner simply needs to claim the business as their own with a button on the business's page. If your business does not yet have a page, there is a button to add a new business in the search page. After claiming the business, there are a few simple questions and an automated phone call to verify that you have access to the business's phone line, so you can't register from home. Once you have access, make sure you fill out your profile page completely. There have been many times I've wanted to go to a restaurant but because its hours weren't listed I assumed they were closed and went somewhere else. After taking the reins and cleaning up your page, the next step is engagement. Take advantage of those local targeted offers, thank people for positive reviews and take the time to respond to negative reviews – constructively. The how and why is covered in detail later.

Yelp also allows mobile business types, like chinese delivery or locksmiths, to specify their range of travel (if they so choose). I wouldn't ever recommend filling this out because there are always exceptions to the rule. I once offered to pay a locksmith double his rate because he was the only one who answered and after talking to him it turned out I was outside of his zone. It was -20 Fahrenheit and windy. I wanted inside. Had I seen his zone on a map before I called, I might not have tried, dismissing him out of hand.

While it's clear that these are great applications for retail and food service businesses, the applicability of mobile check-in applications to professional services is still being worked out. Doctors and lawyers should probably avoid encouraging users to check in, while a CPA might want to give it a shot. As they say over at flyertalk.com: YMMV (or, your millage may vary).

Lingo

Unlike many of the other services out there, Yelp doesn't need much introduction in the way of jargon. Most of its services are based on very traditional concepts, only instead of sourcing experts like the career restaurant reviewer for the local paper, users do the reviews. Foursquare is also relatively simple in that it offers rewards for checking into locations with points. The person with the most check-ins at a location becomes the mayor, Yelp's check in structure is similar. Both services offer badges, which are just signifiers that you've checked into a collection of places. For example, Foursquare offers a Ski Bum Badge, meaning (duh) you're a ski bum. Neither service allows for any real network building for businesses like we see on Facebook or Twitter, and there are no friends lists for businesses. Individual users can interact in a much more social way, but there is a wall of separation between businesses and users that is unique to these services. In fact, Yelp's terms of service bars businesses from normal user accounts for promotional use. While users have forums on Yelp and business owners can respond to comments, there is no real opportunity for sustained dialogue. You can offer promotions here to attract users and encourage people to become regulars, the tools required are more traditional and rely on real world interaction instead of digital communication. Content creation is also limited to promotions, filling out the basic information about your business and responding to the occasional negative review.

Yelp in Person

We already know that if a client has already looked up a store on Yelp before coming in, they are 20% more likely to make a purchase. But Yelp's transition off the computer screen into the real world doesn't end there. Yelp offers stickers to local businesses reading, "People Love Us on Yelp!" Foursquare offers its own version of the same. These stickers reinforce the systems in several ways. First, they remind customers using their mobil devices to check in and review the store. Second, such reviews build awareness of the systems, and the company also benefits because the customer knows it has good reviews on Yelp. To qualify for a sticker, a business just needs an average of 3.5 stars or more and a fair amount of reviews. Yelp sends the stickers out annually, and they are absolutely worth putting up if you receive one.

Yelp also throws parties. Free drinks, free food and free fun. Plus, you get to meet the Elite Squad, a group of Yelp super users who contribute the bulk of the reviews on the network. While I haven't seen data for Yelp, I'd imagine its authorship structure is similar to Wikipedia where a small group of users known as "The Cabal" contributes the lion's share of the writing. Not surprising since Prado's law presupposes that 80% of the content would be generated by 20% of the users. Having these users on your side means you have the opportunity to get reviews from a group of people who take the time to write great reviews. They are a group of people who hold influence over friends and are more likely to be asked by others to recommend a product, which, like many other things, is sure to be good for your standings in search engine results.

One of the most unique aspects of Yelp is just how personable the service is. It threw me for a loop when I had personal contact with a Yelp employee for the first time. She left me with her cell phone number. It was baffling. Unfortunately, Annie wasn't sharing the number with me because she wanted to get dinner and movie. Instead, she was reaching out as the Minneapolis Community Manager. If there is any service or good you can contribute to these parties, it's worth considering. She turned out to be great to work with and a real benefit to the company. With her help, we brought our wares to several Yelp sponsored parties where guests were encouraged to write reviews about our service. Five stars across the board from dozens of reviewers was empirically valuable to the bottom line. Get in touch with your community manager. They are the digital gatekeepers. In a world where you have little power to control what others write about you, they hold a surprising amount of sway and can also help link your brand to Yelp. It's also nice to be able to ask a question about Yelp to a person versus rereading this chapter or searching through online message boards. No, they won't delete bad reviews, but they can help you strategize how to deal with them and how to get better reviews.

Only a quarter of companies surveyed for Econsultancy's customer engagement report tap into user ratings and feedback. This translates into an advantage for you. If you are able to tap into these and encourage and shepherd them (not moderate them), you will have a huge leg up over 75% of your competition. This is about engagement at touch points and reminders: "Check us out on Yelp!" So put your sticker up when you get it.

Mobile Yelp

Yelp is mobile enabled and rolls in many of the features that the Foursquare application boasts. Stores can take advantage of check in offers. When a customer comes to your store and "checks in" with Yelp or Foursquare via their mobile phone, they will instantly receive a coupon. The benefit to you is that those check-ins show up in community news. They also act as a reminder to that customer to later review you in length. Foursquare has some advanced functionality when it comes to offering coupons or deals to customers. In their system, you can set up requirements for a certain number of check-ins before a coupon is activated or requires Mayorship for certain deals.

The Yelp app interfaces with many other layers like Facebook. Foursquare interfaces with Twitter. Users can setup check-ins to be syndicated to their various social media. It's not something I would recommend since it goes against our rules of not using robots. It is also very annoying to Facebook friends. Yelp also interfaces with OpenTable, allowing the user to make reservations at restaurants all over the nation right from the review page. Something I love dearly and take advantage of frequently.

When a user is looking for a local barber and find one that has five stars because the barber has managed his business and his social media well, they have a very high probability of calling the barber right then on the spot from the Yelp application. In fact a phone call is made from the Yelp app every other second.[12] Pretty amazing considering it is only available on the iPhone and the Android.

One feature Foursquare offers that Yelp does not makes it particularly useful for companies that offer loyalty cards. Coffee shops regularly offer specials like "Buy 10 cups, get the 11th free." Loyalty programs like this have demonstrated their ability to keep customers coming back time and time again. But when linked to a service like Foursquare, the customer can check in 10 times to get the same special while also informing all of their friends that they like the coffee shop. Yes, finding out a friend went to the same coffee shop 10 times in a row on Twitter is super annoying. However, the reader won't be annoyed with the coffee shop. They will be annoyed with their friend. They will also remember that coffee shop. There is also the option to reward "Mayorship" or the person who has checked in most times at your company. Mayorship takes advantage of gamesmanship rules and starts a sort of bidding war between users, where one person will check in (purchase goods) to oust another person who holds the Mayorship title. A small reward is all it takes to set off a bidding war and can result in sizable returns from a small group of people.

The Foursquare Dashboard is probably one of the most interesting features to come from the platform. From here you can find out your top customers, most recent check ins and more. You can keep track of your loyal customers and give them the attention they deserve, you can even see if they suddenly disappear and if they are on twitter, shoot them a DM. Snazzy.

---

[12]http://officialblog.yelp.com/2011/02/via-yelp-mobile-yelpers-call-a-local-business-every-other-second.html

Bad Behavior

It may be tempting to shove your laptop under your customers' noses and tell them to write a review of you. It may even be tempting to email every client and say, "Hey! It was great working with you. I'd love it if you could tell us and the world what you thought of your experience with us!" Nope. Not allowed. Not even the second one. How do I know? I was chastised by Annie. Even though I wasn't asking people to write good reviews, it's still against the rules. And because many of our reviews came from first time users, Annie caught onto my not so well concealed, not so clever ruse.

What you can say: "Check us out on Yelp!" Since it's not asking for a review, it's fine according to the Yelp terms of service. While it's definitely going to return fewer reviews to you, it's definitely a valuable thing to include at every possible touch point.

Even if you do openly ask your customers to write reviews, and they do write reviews in your favor, they are going to get filtered. Unless they are already Yelp users, a customer's review is going to be treated as suspicious. That's why mine were filtered. I was having first time customers write glowing reviews. It was flattering because they were taking the time to write long, detailed stories about their positive experiences, but they said it just because I asked them for a review. Sadly, they were filtered because they were all 5 stars and very, very long winded. To Yelp it looked like I was writing the reviews. It's a drag, it's frustrating, but it's handled that way to keep Yelp's credibility high.

I begged Annie to unfilter those reviews, but she refused. I've read since then that she doesn't even have that capability. That's a good thing, I know my Yelp Community Manager isn't crooked, but that is something other managers have been accused of. Those positive reviews were casualties in the war against spam and dishonesty. I know my competitors have had positive reviews removed too, and I've pointed out reviews that were obviously fraudulent. What kind of towing company gets four 5 star reviews in a week? Seriously?

Even thanking customers for positive reviews with special gifts or further comments on positive reviews is frowned upon by Yelp. Instead, if someone say's you're awesome, you should say only "thank you." Nothing more. This is because anything beyond a simple thank you could be misunderstood to be a payment (bribe) for a good review. Responding once in a while to a particularly glowing review is probably a good idea, responding to all good reviews with a thank you is a bit much. Instead, send a private message.

Because of these efforts, Yelp's credibility has remained strong, and they have possibly boosted the credibility of other similar sites across the Internet. According to a recent survey published by the Wall Street Journal, 92% of people have more faith in information about a product they buy online than from a clerk or from another source. I find that pretty astounding.

Dealing with Negative Reviews

Sean C. of San Francisco posted a review on Yelp of a local bookstore, calling the shop "a mess." Later in the day, a woman knocked on his door and tried to force her way into his apartment. The woman turned out to be the store manager, and she was out for revenge. No one knew just how she found Sean, but she did, and she certainly did not do her book store any favors in the PR department.[13] There is another story of a company that started to include in all of their contracts that posting a negative Yelp review was a violation of contract and would be met with legal action. Don't do those things.

Negative reviews are a scary thing, small business owners are even more vulnerable to negative reviews and far more likely to be hurt by them, if not financially then emotionally. After all, for most small business owners, their companies are their babies, and negative reviews feel like personal attacks. But they aren't. They are, in fact, good to have, in moderation of course.

The negative review offers two things. First, the possibility to respond publicly. One could choose to find the negative reviewer and punch them in the face, but that would be sure to highlight your company in a negative light on the six o'clock news. Instead, take a deep breath and decide if you are in a good place to respond to the negative review. Be honest with yourself. Anything short of a constructive and positive comment can make things worse. If you're

---

[13]http://www.nbcbayarea.com/news/local/San-Francisco-Bookstore-Has-an-Uneahlty-Yelp-Confrontation-68914367.html

ready, acknowledge the reviewer and thank them for bringing the situation to your attention, let them know how you will correct the situation and give them a way to personally contact you so you can discuss the problem further. Keep it simple. This lets the reviewer know you care. It lets everyone who reads that review know you care. It signals that the problem won't happen again and shows that you take the situation seriously. It's just as valuable to show that one customer you take quality control seriously as it is to show all other customers that you take the problem seriously. But be careful and keep the response short! It's easy to dig yourself in a hole, seem condescending or seem disingenuous when writing on the Internet. A great example of how to respond would be:

John,
  Thank you for posting this here and bringing your concern to our attention. Please know we have taken steps to ensure that this doesn't happen again. I would love to talk to you and make sure we have fixed the problem completely. You can reach my extension at 555-555-5555.
  Thank you again,
  Chris Sanger

John couldn't misinterpret that as smug, condescending, sarcastic, bullying, rude, short, angry, spiteful, etc. if he tried. That's where you want to be. Feel free to steal that verbatim.

If the reviewer's comments come off as totally crazy, you're probably best just leaving the comment alone. Especially if it's full of bad grammar and misspellings. Attributes such as those result in reviews not being taken seriously anyways and someone that's totally irate and making things up probably doesn't care if you want to fix the problem. Because of this phenomenon Zappo's has famously hired people to go through and fix grammar and spelling on reviews for the site's products, ensuring they are taken seriously.

The second thing the negative review offers is credibility. Everyone knows nothing is perfect, and a huge amount of perfect reviews with no negative reviews starts to trip a bullshit meter in the consumer's mind. A small percentage of reviews signal to the consumer that the reviewers are real people with real experiences, and the small percentage increases their trust in the reviews. A negative review is still a review, so it will increase the total number of reviews you have, and it turns out that sheer numbers are far more important than average stars. After a company or product has 20 reviews, the number of reviews start to grow exponentially, and as numbers grow so do conversion rates. This is most easily observable on Amazon.com, where many very popular books have thousands of user reviews. One might think that reviews would taper off after 1,000 reviews. People would think, "What's the point of writing another review?" But they don't. Reviews beget more reviews. If a reader understands the psychology behind this, please, email me.

Advertising on Yelp

There are two major routes for advertising delivery on Yelp: paid advertising and promotions. Offering a promotion on Yelp or Foursquare gives you a major advantage in search results, as your business name will show up with an icon next to it, indicating that you have a special offer available. The offer need not be large, but it should be a real offer. I have seen businesses list announcements as offers just so they could get the icon. This is deceptive. Listing a special offer also places your business in the "Sales & Special Offers" list, something every good yelper and Foursquare user checks once in a while. This is a low cost method for exposure and a great way to bring some attention to your company. While you shouldn't use the special offer section just to make announcements, it is certainly a good idea to showcase anything new or exciting happening at your company. An example of an effective way to structure a special promotion could be:

"We just remodeled and are excited to show off! Every yelper who visits us gets a free appetizer this week!"

Such offers have certainly gotten me in the door and Foursquare specials have definitely adjusted my purchasing patterns. The loyalty function of these specials is amazingly effective for drawing in repeat customers. $10 off on my 5th visit? I'll take advantage of that.

Yelp also offers paid advertising. The program offers some nice features, like adding a slide show of images and preventing other businesses from showing up on your Yelp page (visitors who liked diner X also liked diner Y). The cost per click is, however, very high when compared to Google advertisements and Facebook advertisements. Also, the ability to hone in on specific data points and their effects on traffic leaves something to be desired. At this point, there just isn't a significant enough reason to pay to advertise when Yelp offers so many great ways to get exposure for free.

Foursquare is still the young pup in the crowd and it seems like every week someone comes up with a new way to use the service for marketing. One of my favorites was a German firm that wired up a billboard to dispense dog food to people that walked by and checked in with their pooches. It was a great campaign since even people that abused the free lunch furthered the ad agency's goal, public exposure of people (dogs) enjoying the product. Making a billboard dispense food is not an easy thing to do, I have no clue how they did this. But certainly, this shows how adaptable the network is. Keep an eye on it, we will do the same.

Hit It!

Twitter and Facebook are so powerful because they mimic the kinds of social transactions we've had for centuries. These location-based services promise to be just as powerful if not more for the same reasons. Where Facebook and Twitter diverge from the kinds of interactions we are used to, Foursquare and Yelp bring us one step closer to adding a layer over traditional social life instead of adding a parallel layer. Instead of a user sitting at home interacting with a computer screen, the user is in the real world interacting with brick and mortar establishments.

These conversations are already taking place. Whether you are there to facilitate them and nurture them is up to you. The tools are out there. They are powerful, and they are in everyone's pockets. They are still the new kids on the block and they haven't finished growing up, but they are capable of great things. Enabling users to interact with you on these systems, by means of coupons, check-ins or Mayorship, is to enable your users to evangelize your brand. They are free, too.

SECTION V

WRAPPING IT UP

Dig in. Go Further.

There will undoubtedly be missteps as you set out to develop your company's social media assets. Hopefully there won't be too much confusion. That's why you bought this book, after all. If there is anything that is unclear, anything you disagree with, send us a tweet. We're experts, but we got that way by listening.

This is a field that is constantly evolving. That's why we've set up a blog at www.cloutsmiths.com. There you can have access to all the latest social media news as it relates to your business. We probably won't break any stories – that's not what we are about. Instead, the site offers a collection of essays about trends and developments in social media that you can use to make money.

Social media has changed the field of advertising. There is no going back to a time where audiences are willing to listen to lectures from companies looking to move product. Instead, businesses and marketers now have to concentrate on having conversations. Consumers and their friends conversing publicly about great brands is more valuable to the brand than traditional advertising anyway, so why would you want to go back?

Social Media is hands on and it's social. These are traits of entrepreneurs, as a small business owner you have the tools needed to succeed. So dive in and explore.

There is just one point I've made throughout this book that I want to leave you with, just in case you never return to these pages. Social media is just an extension of our real world customs and norms (and taboos). No matter what you do on Facebook or Twitter, ask yourself if it's something you would say to a client if they were in your store. Ask yourself if you're asking a reasonable question. Ask yourself, "Will this offend anyone?" Ask "is this awesome?" Asking these questions and motivating yourself to stay productive are the two keys to success on any social media platform, even the ones that haven't been invented yet.

Dig in, don't ever be discouraged, have fun and be awesome.

Christopher Sanger

ABOUT THE AUTHOR

Chris Sanger is the founder of The Clout Smiths, a company dedicated to enabling small business owners to create and maintain their own in-house social media campaigns. Over the years, Sanger has worked for a handful of small businesses, some of which have grown very large, building their social media strategies. After one of these companies grew sufficiently large enough for Sanger to start teaching others to use Facebook and Twitter, he decided to set out on his own.

An urban planning geek, just like the founder of Twitter, Sanger approaches social media in a way that is relatable to anyone, even if they've never used a computer before. By examining social media through the language of cities and human relationships, he defines Facebook and Twitter in familiar and easy to understand ways, along with revealing some useful and new ideas about each of those services.

Sanger lives in Minneapolis, Minnesota, with his girlfriend Julianna and their dogs, Laika and Loki.

Made in the USA
Charleston, SC
22 June 2012